BREAK EVERY CHAIN

A police officer's battle with alcoholism, depression, and devastating
loss; and the true story of how God changed his life forever.

Jonathan E. Hickory

ISBN 978-1-64300-756-4 (Paperback)
ISBN 978-1-64300-757-1 (Digital)

Covenant Books, Inc.
11661 Hwy 707
Murrells Inlet, SC 29576
www.covenantbooks.com

For Stacy, Ana, and Zachariah

Praise for

Break Every Chain

"How often does a memoir open with the author describing himself as *a monster*: emotionally absent, mean to his wife and young daughter, hung over, full of hatred for himself and life? That's the picture Jonathan Hickory vividly paints in *Break Every Chain*. Right off the bat Jonathan nails why his life was such a train wreck – from trying in vain "to fill the void in our souls and hearts with empty promises and lies from Satan." With remarkable transparency and vulnerability, Jonathan walks us through his seasons of addiction, abuse, destruction and infidelity. And then – the breakthrough – God's mercy, grace and power reaching down and transforming him from the inside out. Jonathan's story will give courage to anyone who fears that their past defines them forever. And for all the heartbroken people who love those wandering souls, it will bring hope that no one is too far gone – not when our Good Shepherd, the Lord Jesus Christ, is out to find His lost sheep. *Break Every Chain* was a pleasure to read. I'm encouraged just imagining how it will minister to everyone looking for restoration and a renewed hope of being fruitful for the kingdom of God."

– **JANICE CAPPUCCI**, author of *Storm Clouds of Blessings: True Stories of Ordinary People Finding Hope and Strength in Times of Trouble*

"A real life story that inspires, encourages, and gives hope—a hope that forgiveness and restoration are possible, even in the darkest of situations."

- **VERNON BREWER**, World Help, Founder/CEO and author of *Defining Moments* and *WHY? Answers to Weather the Storms of Life*

"Uplifting! Jonathan's story is gut wrenching and triumphant at the same time. He lays his soul bare and leaves you with immense gratitude for the sacrifices that our law enforcement officers and their loved ones make."

- **ERIK SABISTON**, author of *Dustoff 7-3, Saving Lives Under Fire in Afghanistan*

"I have always told people being a cop is the hardest job they'll never understand. You have to put your personal feelings in a bottle before your shift and hope that bottle doesn't break open while you're working. I was motivated and captivated by what I was reading… Jonathan's trials and tribulations make for a compelling and powerful story!

-**CHRIS BARCOMB**, retired Police Officer and author of *The Amazing Adventure of Superior Sam*

"In the face of every difficult moment in life, we are left with two distinct choices. We can rise to the occasion with strength, courage and hope; or we can spiral out of control in defeat. In his book *Break Every Chain*, Jonathan Hickory has written about his journey and how God led him from defeat to victory through the power of the Gospel. This is a gripping real story that will give us all the encouragement we need to face whatever might lie ahead in our journey, and to do so with hope."

-**JONATHAN FALWELL**, Senior Pastor, Thomas Road Baptist Church, Lynchburg, Virginia and author of *One Great Truth: Finding Your Answers to Life*

"I could not put this down and read it in one sitting! The compelling testimony of this decorated cop's cop will break your hard heart—as most of us cops will see ourselves—but will leave you with the path to heal your broken heart. Jonathan's transparency gives hope to the hopeless and a message of salvation to those who are lost. This is a must read."

-**PAUL LEE** Capt. Chattanooga PD (Ret.), Executive Director, Fellowship of Christian Peace Officers-USA

"Society as a whole has overlooked and underappreciated the brave men and women who patrol our streets. These people behind the badge have hurts, fears, and frustrations just like anyone else, but unlike everyone else, must carry on as if they were a machine without feeling or recourse. In Jonathan's book, *Break Every Chain* we get a glimpse into the all-too-familiar struggles brewing within one of these brave warriors. Thankfully, he found the secret to breaking through the darkness. It is my prayer that you, too, will come to the realization that there *is* a way out and this vicious cycle *can* be changed, and your life *can* be healed from the inside out. He's just waiting for you to call on Him. His name is Jesus!

-**KRISTI NEACE**, Founder, Badge of Hope Ministries, Police wife/mom, Speaker, author of numerous books including *Under Fire: Marriage Through the Eyes of a Cop's Wife.*

In *Break Every Chain,* Officer Jonathan Hickory paints a vivid picture of the unique issues we who serve in our God-ordained (Romans 13:1-4) profession of law enforcement face both personally and professionally. More importantly, Jonathan points us both to what ails us in our calling and to "the Cure" – a genuine, life-saving/life-changing personal relationship with the greatest "cop" in history – Jesus Christ. Jonathan's book is both a warning and – praise God – a testimony of hope that should be "must reading" for every officer, police spouse and, frankly, every man. Highly recommended!

-MICHAEL "MC" WILLIAMS, Police Officer and Chaplain, Founder and Director, The Centurion Law Enforcement Ministry

"Jonathan Hickory takes the reader down a dark, twisted, and at times, death defying journey which miraculously leads to redemption. *Break Every Chain* epitomizes the personal struggles of many law enforcement officers, the real battle between good and evil, and how the power of God can set the captives free. A MUST READ!"

-REV. MARCOS A. MIRANDA, DMin., BCC
President, New York State Chaplain Task Force
Chaplain, New York State Fraternal Order of Police

"Wow. A riveting account of pain and redemption. A painful and empowering narrative of a hero's journey into darkness, and the power of God to lead him home. Telling us again, in a modern context, that critical, life-affirming lesson: "It is no secret, what God can do. What He's done for others, He can do for you."

-LT. COL. DAVE GROSSMAN, author of *On Combat, On Killing* and *Assassination Generation*

"The night is nearly over; the day is almost here. So let us put aside the deeds of darkness and put on the armor of light."

(Romans 13:12 NIV)

Contents

Foreword

I'll never forget the first time I met Jonathan. He was seated with his wife Stacy about two-thirds of the way back in the middle section of our auditorium. Jonathan and Stacy were there early for our church service, but this wasn't unusual for Stacy. She had been attending our church for some time.

Because they were early, there was not a sea of people to make my way through to reach them to say good morning. I said hi to Stacy and then introduced myself to Jonathan. As we spoke, Jonathan's responses were respectful but short, which clearly communicated to me, "Leave me alone."

At the time I knew nothing of the deep pain and loss that Jonathan had experienced in his life, nor the struggles that he and Stacy were currently facing. Behind our short greeting and conversation was a story—the story of a man who was very much broken and in desperate need of Jesus and the forgiveness and healing that are only found in Him.

In this book, *Break Every Chain*, Jonathan vulnerably takes us through his own beautifully told journey of pain, loss, darkness, desperation, forgiveness, healing, and restoration.

If you are struggling with questions about the existence or reality of God, or you have found yourself shackled by addictions or other forms of bondage, *Break Every Chain* is a powerful message of hope, reminding us of the life-changing power of the Gospel of Jesus Christ. *Break Every Chain* illustrates this beautiful truth: regardless of how low we find ourselves, there is always hope in Him.

After reading Jonathan's story, I found that it spoke to and encouraged my heart, serving as a much needed reminder—every person you meet has a story. The story within so many hearts is a story that includes brokenness, bondage, and chains from which they need to be freed. This freedom is only found in the Gospel that we are called to live and preach.

Gabe Turner
Senior Pastor, The Point Church,
Charlottesville, Virginia

Introduction

I am sitting with my wife, Stacy, and my five-year-old daughter, Ana, in the middle of Walt Disney World. It is April 2015. We are having breakfast at the Animal Kingdom Resort, and I am hung over again from drinking in the hotel room last night while my family slept. The rum and vodka cocktail is still strong on my breath as I struggle to maintain interest while we discuss the agenda for the day. I stare blankly at the nearby pool, poking at the runny eggs on my plate.

I should be having a wonderful time with my family. I should be enjoying the magic of this animated adventure park like when I was a kid. Instead, I am lost in my own misery and darkness. I feel worthless. I am so tired of feeling tired and I hate who I am. I say something disrespectful and condescending to my wife, snapping at her as she tries to include me in our family's plans.

"I hate you." Stacy's stinging words get my attention.

"What?" Like I didn't hear her.

"*I hate you!* Everything you ever say is mean, and we don't deserve to be treated like this! We are your *family!*"

Stacy had tears in her eyes. Of course she meant it. Instead of lashing back, I pondered her words for a moment, and it was almost as if someone had finally flipped a switch. I felt like I had been slapped in the face. But she was *right*. Something needed to change. I was a monster and I was destroying my life and hers.

This is a story of hope. It is a story of God working in my life to save me and to change me forever. I am writing this story because I realize that we are all broken and we all have our hardships and trials in life. Without God, we all will try to fill the void in our souls and hearts with empty promises and lies from Satan.

This is a real story with real pain, loss, suffering, and heartache. This is a story about addiction, abuse, destruction, and infidelity. This is also a story about obedience, redemption, freedom, restoration, and true love. You will see the power of evil and how Satan tried to destroy me and my family. You will see the amazing power of God restoring my once lost and broken soul through His never-ending love. This is my story and I wish that it was more perfect than it is. My prayer is that God is glorified through this book, that it will give you a sense of hope, and that you would open your heart to our heavenly Father.

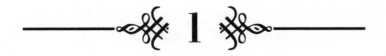

Dad

My mother called Sarah and I over to come sit on her lap in the big, comfy armchair that Dad always sat in. It was January 1991 in small town Rutland, Massachusetts. As Sarah and I fought for space in the well-worn chair, a sudden quiet and stillness came over my mother. Even at the age of eleven, I knew my mother was fighting back something that was bothering her. My sister, Sarah, was only nine and she was very sweet. She had no idea to expect the devastating words that would soon pass into her ears and shatter her innocence forever. Sarah's dark brown hair and darker brown eyes burrowed into Mom's soft navy blue sweatshirt as she seemed to begin to sense that something was wrong.

To this day, I admire my mother's faith during that time. Her calm spirit knew that God was in control, even in a time of tragedy and sadness. I cannot imagine how she could tell her children such dreadful news and also be so comforting in the same moment. If my mother did not have her faith, I do not know where I would be today. That is the amazing power of Jesus Christ.

The words slammed into my ears like a freight train barreling into a tunnel. "Daddy is sick. God is going to be taking him home soon." Mom spoke softly and calmly as she tried to explain to her youngest two children that her husband of twenty-two years, the father of her four children, had terminal cancer. I tried to ask questions, but the confusion and the anger I felt soon was choked out by burning, unstoppable tears. I hid my face in the darkness of the back of the chair, not believing this could be reality. Sarah and I sobbed together with Mom for over an hour as the sun began to cast shadows on the chilly New England afternoon.

Just a few hours ago, I was a care-free sixth grader. A few hours ago, my biggest worry was when the book report was due for Mrs. Keaton's class. A few hours ago, my father was okay. We were all okay. Now my father was dying. Now my mother was going to be a widow. Now I didn't understand why this was happening to our family. Now I was angry. How could this be real? Why would God take away my dad? Didn't God know that we needed him? That I needed him?

My dad was a genius. I am biased, but really, it's true! Gordon Everett Hickory was an engineer in abrasive technologies. He was a professor at Tufts University early in his career. Later, he engineered things like grinding wheels and sandpaper. I had to throw sandpaper in there, because I am not really sure what a grinding wheel is or what it does. Dad even had his name on a few US patents in the abrasives industry and was the most brilliant guy I knew… not that I knew that many people as an eleven year old kid. He made a good living and took great care of us four kids and he loved us very much.

Even though she was a registered nurse, my mother was able to stay at home and raise us while Dad supported us. Dad was an elder in The Immanuel Chapel Church in Upton, Massachusetts, and I would often admire watching him take up the offering with the other elders. Dad drove a humongous blue Oldsmobile Delta 88 sedan and liked his American vehicles. Dad collected antique guns, and I remember he loved to watch (with me at his side) all sorts of westerns, including John Wayne movies and classics like *Gunsmoke* and *Bonanza*.

Dad was serious but sometimes was silly with us. I remember he gave me an allowance of $2.00 a week—pretty good money back then—which I usually squandered on penny candy and baseball cards at the Rutland Pharmacy. I did have to do chores to earn the allowance, so don't think I had it too easy! Most importantly, Dad loved my mom. I never remember them fighting or arguing in any way. Mom and Dad held God above all in their marriage, and it showed in their love for each other and their love for us.

When I was nine years old, Dad bought me a bow and arrow set for my birthday. It was a black colored Browning Fox Compound Bow, complete with a camouflage quiver and arrows. I even got a little glove to protect my fingers. I remember spending hours and hours practicing with that bow and arrow. It was the best gift I had ever received! It made me so proud that my dad gave me such a coveted present. I felt like a true sportsman when I would draw back on the string, take aim, and release arrow after arrow into the Styrofoam target.

One night, before my dad got sick, I was getting ready to go to bed. I was very proud of myself because I had just learned the old rhyme *Fuzzy Wuzzy*. I was probably eight or nine at the time. You may remember the rhyme. "Fuzzy Wuzzy was a bear. Fuzzy Wuzzy had no hair. Fuzzy Wuzzy wasn't very fuzzy, was he?"

I loved that rhyme so much! I recited it proudly to Dad. My father looked at me and, without warning, recited his own rendition of the rhyme: "Scuzzy Wuzzy was a bear, Scuzzy Wuzzy had no hair… Scuzzy Wuzzy wasn't very scuzzy, was he?"

We both laughed. It felt good to laugh with my dad. I knew he loved me, and that felt good.

A few years before we found out that our father was going home to be with the Lord, Dad lost his job with a prominent Worcester, Massachusetts-based abrasive company called Norton Company. Four children plus no income equals not good. Thankfully, Dad found another job working for another company, Bay State Abrasives.

With my father on their team, Bay State Abrasives began to do very well (I told you he was a genius)! Norton Company apparently wasn't a fan of this newfound success by Bay State Abrasives, and so Norton Company decided it might be a swell idea to sue Bay State Abrasives *and* my dad for millions of dollars for allegedly stealing trade secrets. What made the idea even more heartfelt? This was while my father was attempting to prolong his life through chemotherapy and radiation, fighting the cancer the best he could with the treatment available back in 1991. This is why I could never be a lawyer! It seemed so wrong to me that anyone could kick my dad while he was already down.

I remember going to court once with Dad while he fought to clear his good name before the cancer pulled all of the life from his ever-weakening body. The marble steps of the courthouse just seemed to make a cold place colder. It was a gray December of 1991, and time was running out for my dad. He had already lost all of his full gray hair and was losing so much weight that, at times, I did not recognize him. Dad had tried wearing a wig for a while to hide his hair loss, but eventually he gave up on the strange looking hairpiece. My father was reduced to complete baldness, and it terrified me to look upon this decrepit version of a man who I loved so dearly.

The trial went on for what seemed like months. One time, Dad was testifying in court and he had to leave the stand prematurely to go vomit because of the chemotherapy sickness. Dad tried his best to be brave for us four children, but he seemed to be weaker with every passing day.

On Monday, December 23, 1991, a Worcester, Massachusetts, superior court jury delivered the verdict, rejecting Norton's claims. Norton Company, one of the city's largest private employers, lost the lawsuit that sought to drag my father's good name (and our family) through the mud! A feeling of relief washed over my father and my family. Dad had less than sixty days to live. I think Dad knew he could go home to be with God. The fight was over.

I don't know what ever happened to Bay State Abrasives. I don't believe they still exist today. I remember that my father was presented with an "Employee of the Year Award" that the company would later entitle "The Gordon E. Hickory Employee of the Year Award" in his honor. Kind of cool. I also remember that once Bay State Abrasives' corporate parent company found out that Dad was sick, they paid for our family to take one last trip together, all expenses paid. Where did we go? Disney World, of course! It was wonderful, but it was sad at the same time. The time together was bittersweet, for all of us knew that it would be the last family vacation we would ever have with Dad. To the former owners or operators of Bay State Abrasives, wherever you are, thank you from the bottom of my heart.

We wheeled my father's gaunt, cancer-ridden body into our colonial-era family home for the last time. Mom took care of him at home for a couple of months with some help from us kids. I try not to remember this part of my life, to block it out. Isn't it strange how we can see things so vividly that we wish we could erase forever? Mom had to keep turning Dad in the bed so he wouldn't get bed sores. I helped out where I could.

I was twelve now, and so that meant I should be able to handle emptying my father's urine bottle. I still don't know how I wound up with that job, but it was mine, and if it meant helping Dad, I was determined not to complain. Mom would later tell me that she gave all the children a chore that somehow involved going in to see my dad so that he wouldn't become "the man in the room" that we were afraid to visit. At the time, I wasn't exactly cheering on the idea, but now I realize she meant it for a greater good.

I would run in and see the old recycled Ocean Spray bottle filled with yellow liquid, and I could not help but stare at my father, a ghostly shadow of his former self as he lay on the bed, barely able to move. The cancer had run its course. I wanted to tell him that everything would be okay. I wanted to tell him how much I loved him and how he couldn't leave me because I needed him! But all I was able to squeak out was a barely audible "I love you" to my father. I remember how it felt so final, like this was the only chance I would get to tell him. I wanted to save him. I wanted to make my daddy the strong man he used to be. The dad that used to take me to gun shows, just me and him. The dad that would take Sarah and me on walks in the woods and take us fishing. The dad that would test the ice for us before we could go ice-skating on the frozen pond behind our house. The dad that could easily pick me up in his strong arms. The dad that would take care of me.

Every night, I would pray, "God, please make my dad better. Please, God, don't take my dad." One night, I would not have to pray for God to heal my father anymore. As children, we wonder about God. I thought of God as a silent, large man with a white beard who looked down on me as I prayed to Him from my bed. For some reason, I thought He didn't want to listen to me. I pleaded with God and I begged, a twelve-year-old boy doing everything he knew to keep his dad.

On the cold Tuesday morning of February 18, 1992, Dad took his last breath and went to be with Jesus in heaven. He was only forty-nine years old. He had fought for thirteen months when the doctors said he would be gone in six. He had cleared his good name. He had given his four children and his loving wife a little more precious time with him. He died while we slept peacefully early that morning. When I awoke, I don't know how I knew; but I knew.

When Mom came in to tell me that Dad was gone, somehow I already felt that he was gone. Blind with anger and tears, I asked my mother if I could say goodbye to Dad because I didn't get to say goodbye. My mother said to me, "Honey, it's just a shell now. Daddy is in heaven." It didn't make it hurt any less. I thought of my father's body lying in the bed, lifeless, just a shell. My life was changed forever. *This is God's fault*, I thought. I prayed and prayed and prayed to Him, and He still took my dad.

My mind raced with thoughts of the future without a dad. Who would teach me to drive? Who would come to my baseball games? Who would pay the bills? Who would take care of our family? Who would take care of my mom? *Dad? Please don't be gone.* That night, and for many, many nights after that, I cried myself to sleep.

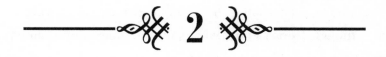

Farms

Kaa-duk kaduk. Kaa-duk kaduk.

The soothing sound of the Amtrak passenger train calmed me for a moment as I stared out the window at the endless scenery whizzing by. It was two months after my father had died. My mother, April (my older sister), and Sarah were taking a trip to see some old family friends who lived in Virginia. I didn't know anything about Virginia. I remember looking out the window of the train, and the Virginia creeks and rivers were all swelling and even flooding from April rains. The water looked like the river in *Willy Wonka and the Chocolate Factory*. I would later learn that this was because of the prominent red clay that makes up the Virginia soil. I thought about how it might be fun to jump into the chocolate water! My mind flashed to the scene from the movie where the boy falls into the chocolate river and is drowning in the sweet gooey liquid. Lately, I felt like I was drowning too with the overwhelming pain in my heart.

We had a memorial service after Dad passed away. It was at the Immanuel Chapel where our family went to church, and Dad was an elder. The tall white steeple loomed overhead as I made my way inside with my mom, my two sisters, and my older brother. I remember that one of my cousins (who I had never met before) sang at the service, though I don't know what song she sang. I also remember all the stares and the heartfelt things that people would say to try to help me feel better, accompanied by awkward pats on the back or the shoulder. Nothing they said seemed to help take away my sadness and anger. Already I was beginning to feel like I was empty inside, like I was lost in darkness.

The memorial service, the required appearance before these people, all seemed like a formality; something our family had to go through. I did my best to put on my brave face. When the organ began to play "Amazing Grace," I lost my ability to be tough. I let the pain and sadness show as I tried to cover my eyes and hide the tears. "I once was lost, but now I'm found," everyone sang while I wept. I didn't feel like I would ever be found.

It was fun taking the train. I had never ridden one before. There was something about passing through the cities and the countryside in the train car that made me feel like a prestigious world traveler, getting a glimpse of people's lives and homes as I passed in and out of their existence. The bright fields and mysterious woods, busy cities, towns, and bridges passed by. The cows and horses of all different colors and varieties seemed to ignore the flash of noisy silver metal cars clattering by.

All I knew is that we were taking a trip to visit some long-time friends of the family. The actual purpose of the trip, I would later discover, was for my mother to interview for a pediatric nursing job at the University of Virginia hospital. Mom was struggling to find a job in Massachusetts, despite her best efforts. She needed a way to support her children, and without our father, her options were limited. I wasn't crazy about the idea of moving. It was hard enough enduring what we had gone through. I didn't need a new zip-code to go with it.

Bert and Bill Stauff had a rustic pastel yellow farmhouse on a few acres of land in Crimora, Virginia. After rattling down what seemed like an endless dirt road, an opening in the wooded wilderness led to this peaceful paradise, complete with pastures filled with tall grasses and thistles and even a small fishing pond!

Oh, how I loved to fish! During the last year of my father's life, I think I fished every single one of the ponds in the town of Rutland. For me, fishing was a way to escape temporarily from reality. All I needed was to get down onto the shore and cast out and I could forget about the world for a little while. All I used to dream about was catching big fish.

One of the beauties of small New England townships is that you can ride your bicycle almost anywhere in town. As an eleven-year-old boy, I eagerly pedaled my way to a different pond every day. I even mastered the technique of riding with a tackle box hung on one side of my handlebars and a fishing pole somehow balanced across the bars as well. I'm really not sure how I did it without crashing. I don't think I could pull that off now! Well, maybe...

Mom must have done really well in her interview. The next thing I knew, we were moving far, far away from my childhood home, church, school, friends, my beloved grandparents, fishing ponds, teachers, Rutland Pizza, and everything and everyone I knew. As I wrapped up my seventh grade in school, I bragged to all my friends that we were moving to Virginia. I tried to pretend that it was something awesome that I was going to do and acted as if my friends should be jealous that they weren't all moving too.

There was a part of me that was excited to move, don't get me wrong. I envisioned being the cool new kid in my new school, all the girls lined up to date me (because you know, so many girls want to date boys in seventh grade). I tried to imagine a new house and a new start. Maybe this would be good for our family. Maybe this was just what we needed—to forget the memories and the reality of things.

In my heart, though, I was scared. I didn't want to leave. I didn't want to make new friends! The ones I had were just fine. There was no way the fishing in Virginia, which all the kids in school decided to call "land of the virgins," would be as good as the fishing here! And it wasn't like we were moving an hour away or even a few hours away. I would now be almost twelve hours from my life as I knew it.

On Memorial Day weekend, 1992, three months after Dad died, we started our journey away to Virginia. We drove down with a few boxes of clothes, and my brother stayed in Massachusetts with the house while we waited for it to sell. My brother, Michael, was twenty-two years old at the time. Mike had a fiancée in Rutland, so he wasn't planning on moving down anytime soon anyway.

My brother and I didn't have the closest relationship at that time since we were born almost ten years apart. Although we weren't very close, I always looked up to Mike. One of the many jobs he held as a young man was a security officer for Pinkerton Security. To a young boy like me, he looked just like a police officer in his light blue shirt and his dark blue perfectly creased pants with light blue stripes on the sides. He even carried one of those big batons, presumably to whack bad guys with. I remember seeing him in his uniform and wanting to be just like him, with his shiny silver badge and his flashlight. He drove the coolest car (a Volkswagen Scirocco) and was the coolest guy I knew.

When Mike was nineteen years old, he was driving his Scirocco in the snow, taking my sister, April, to school. A full-sized Chevrolet Blazer lost control and started coming toward my brother's car head on. At the last minute, Mike swerved and took the full impact in the driver's door, saving April's life. It was a horrid crash. April said that after the crash, she was holding Mike's head in her lap as he lay slumped over her, spitting out glass. Mike was in the hospital for over two months and had to have several surgeries after the crash. Later, he would try to join the military, but none of the armed forces would take him because he had permanent metal screws in his arm. I thank God that Michael is still here on Earth with me today.

While we searched for a home in the Charlottesville, Virginia area, we rented a cottage on a cattle farm out in a small area called White Hall. Bill Stauff had seen a listing for the rental cottage on the bulletin board at the church they attended in Charlottesville. I didn't know it at the time, but this was God at work. Don and Sheila Richardson were the owners of Dunrovin Farm, and they were a wonderful, joyful, godly couple who welcomed us into their lives and also invited us to attend their church.

It just so happened that the Richardsons had a boy about my age named Scott. The best thing about Scott, I decided immediately, other than his love of *Teenage Mutant Ninja Turtles*, was the fact that he had a Nintendo Entertainment System. Oh, and Scott also had a Super Nintendo! Looking back at it now, I feel bad that I spent so much time hanging out with my new friend while my younger sister, Sarah, had no friends to play with. I was a selfish kid back then and I really wasn't too concerned with what Sarah was doing at the time. When Scott and I weren't rotting our brains playing endless video games like *The Legend of Zelda* and *Super Mario Brothers*, we did play together outside, and Sarah was able to join us.

Across from our tiny farm cottage (which for bonus points had no air conditioning, shaky electricity, and a copperhead snake living in the crawl space) was a small fishing pond. Maybe this situation wasn't so bad after all! There was a little rowboat complete with some sort of paddle sitting next to the pond. Not long after we moved in, I decided it was time to assess the fishing quality of this pond and the seaworthiness of the boat. I dug out the fishing pole I had brought with me from Rutland and readied my sea legs (or pond legs). Braving the tall grass growing up around the boat, I made my way to the proud vessel.

The boat was a metal skiff and had been placed upside down, presumably to prevent rain water from collecting within the boat. It was heavier than I thought it would be, but after a little muscle, I was able to flip the boat over. Unbeknownst to me, I had just disturbed the resting place of a six (or maybe eight or ten) foot long, slithering, completely evil, definitely plotting against me, scaly, disgusting black snake. I leapt into the air approximately eight feet, and when I came back down, I took off running for my dear life. At the time, I had no clue that black snakes are (allegedly) harmless. All snakes were evil and full of poisonous venom in my book. Let's just say I reached the decision not to go fishing that day. Before you make fun of me, remember that Indiana Jones was afraid of snakes too!

Living on that farm in the summer of 1992 was just what my family needed. Never having set foot on a real farm for very long, we loved the adventures that awaited us anew each morning. We would watch the cows beat the heat as they went for a dip in the pond and take great thrill in trying to catch the fireflies at dusk.

Mom had quickly begun her job as a nurse at the hospital, and she was working night shift. That meant that at night, we were alone in the house—just April, Sarah, and me. During the day, Mom would come home in the morning and have to sleep all day. She was so exhausted. I don't know how Mom did it. I work night shift for the police department, and it is not always easy. I know that my world had been turned upside down when my dad died and turned upside down again when we moved away to Virginia. As a child, you don't always realize the selfless sacrifices your parents make for you. I realize now that my world being turned upside down was nothing compared to my mom's world being overturned.

Soon the summer would come to an end, our new home would be ready for us to move in, our time on Dunrovin Farm would end, and it would be time to start a new school. Although our family only lived on that farm with Don and Sheila Richardson a few months, the memories of that summer and my relationship with the Richardson family will last forever. Over the past twenty-five years, the Richardson family continued to be a part of my life at all of the most crucial steps. I did not know it at the time, but when I met the Richardson family, I was meeting some of my first appointed Earthly guardian angels.

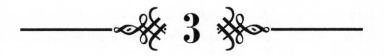

New School

We found a house to move into that was about halfway between Dunrovin Farm and the new school we would be attending. As a matter of fact, the new house was *directly* on the way to our new school from the Richardson's farm. This was *God at work*.

When I say that the Richardson family were my guardian angels, I don't say it lightly. When it was time for Sarah and me to start a new school that fall (April had just graduated high school before we moved), they helped my mother to enroll us in a private Christian school that their son, Scott, was attending. With my mother working night shift at the hospital, it would be impossible for her to get us to school on time each morning, and there were no buses. Don and Sheila Richardson took turns picking Sarah and me up in the mornings and took us home in the afternoons every day after school. They continued to provide us with transportation to and from school for three years until I began driving myself in the eleventh grade. They never asked for gas money and they never complained. These were God's people doing His work.

The school that Sarah and I began attending in the fall of 1992 is called The Covenant School. It really was a wonderful school and still is to this day. From the moment I began my first day of class, I felt welcome. The building itself wasn't the most inviting; the school was an old public high school that was built in the 1930s and still had most of the original construction from that time period. Covenant had only opened its doors seven years prior and so they were still starting out. The school was cold in the winter and roasting hot in the warmer months. But that didn't matter much as the staff was Christ-centered and therefore the most loving, caring, and genuine people I had ever been around.

I made a few friends, but for the most part, I felt like I didn't belong, even though the teachers were so amazing at my new school. I was "cool" and popular in my old school, and now I felt like a nerd who didn't fit in with anyone. The one kid that did genuinely befriend me was an African American young man named Gabe. I remember him being incredibly smart, and he had just moved to the area as well after spending some time with his family in the mission field in Haiti. We both liked Civil War history and we liked to draw. We would draw little cartoons of epic battles taking place between the Union and the Confederacy, and we would always make the Union win. The cartoons that I drew started to get pretty violent as I would draw deceased soldiers with swords sticking out of them and things like that. I found pleasure in drawing these violent scenes, and although I thought it was pretty normal at the time, this was probably one of the ways I was dealing with my impressions and idea of death.

My last day of eighth grade ended on a bad note. I don't remember why, but I had some sort of beef with another kid who was two years behind me but much bigger than I was. Funny how it works like that. I'll call him Melvin. During lunchtime in between my final exams, somehow Melvin and I found ourselves staring each other down in the cafeteria.

Mysteriously all the teachers vanished, and as the tumbleweeds blew past, another kid who apparently wasn't having an exciting enough day pushed me into Melvin. As I tumbled into Melvin, he drew back and landed the most powerful punch I had ever experienced, right on my forehead! I was so dazed that I just kind of stood there in some sort of pathetic fighting stance, holding my fists up but never advancing on Melvin. He had cleaned my clock and I didn't even pick a fight with him! No further blows were exchanged, but I did have a nice souvenir on my temple from being clobbered.

An hour later, as I tried to concentrate on my final History exam, my head was pounding and I would gingerly reach up and feel the huge knot on my head, hoping no one could tell that I had been struck. It wasn't the best way to end the school year, but at least I passed the History exam. And so began summertime.

Don Richardson was a well-respected dermatologist. He was also a well-known teacher in the church, and he and his wife, Sheila, would teach classes together on creationism. Dr. Richardson was also a farmer. He had roughly one hundred head of Polled Hereford cows on Dunrovin Farm. Don knew that Sarah and I did not have a father, and we needed a positive, godly male role model in our lives. I craved it, really, and I know Sarah did too. It wasn't on Mom's heart to remarry or even to date anyone; she knew it would be too hard on us kids. Besides, I don't think Mom had any desire to start over after being married to Dad for over twenty-three years.

One day, Don invited Sarah and me over to the farm. He told us he had something to show us. His son, Scott, walked with us as we made our way over to the barn in the summer heat. Inside one of the fenced areas around the barn, there were three heifers. To you city folk who don't know what a heifer is, don't feel bad, because neither did I! A heifer is a female cow who has not yet had any babies. Don walked into the barn and instructed us to fill a bucket with grain. Cows love grain, and sometimes they will eat it right out the bucket while you are holding it! When we had filled the bucket with sweet grain as instructed, Don grabbed three halters and told us that we were going to halter train these cows.

I was a bit confused at this point. I understand why people would train horses to be ridden. But what in the world was the idea behind training a cow to walk on a leash? It was explained to me that people actually show cows in competitions, and in order to show the cows, they needed to be trained to walk while someone led them around. It was further explained to me that Sarah, Scott, and I were to be the people showing these animals. Don Richardson thought it would be a swell idea for us to learn how to perform this preposterous task!

Despite my reservations, good ole' Dr. Richardson could be quite convincing and could talk most anyone into anything. God had certainly blessed him in the ability to win folks over with his smooth talking logic and quick wit. He taught us all the skills needed to properly show these heifers. Don took care of registering us at a few Beef Expos and even the County Fair and the State Fair. He showed us how to wash the cows, clip their coats, walk them around a show ring on a lead, and position their feet using a long stick with a hook that looked like some sort of whaling harpoon. When we went to shows and fairs, we took the cows with us on a trailer that Don pulled with his pickup truck. Don would also teach me how to hook up a trailer and how to drive a manual transmission on that old truck.

I named my cow Curdles. Like curdled milk, get it? I thought it was clever. Sarah called her cow Molly, and Scott called his cow Brisket. We had a lot of fun learning how to tame these meandering beasts. I learned the value of steel-toed boots and learned its best not to stand behind a cow who just might take a shot at you with its hooves. It was a great way for us kids to stay out of trouble and bond with each other.

Don Richardson appreciated God's creation and taught us a lot about the outdoors and farm life. God bless him for what he did. In a world of men who are so career-focused and self-absorbed, Dr. Richardson gave us a lot of his time and his love to give us hope at a time when we needed it so desperately.

There was a day that I was getting Curdles the cow ready for a big show (yes, there are big events in the world of showing cattle) and I needed to wash her manure-covered coat. I was bent over with my head down trying to scrub a spot just forward of Curdles' rear leg. I know what you are thinking... this doesn't sound like it's going to have a happy ending. Curdles must have thought that the brush was a horsefly landing on her or she just wanted to get her revenge on me for all those times I had led her around in circles. She suddenly kicked and landed her hoof on the left side of my head, bending the glasses I was wearing, and stunning me for a few minutes. As I gathered my consciousness (and my glasses), I remember thinking how ungrateful Curdles was for kicking me while I was trying to give her a bath! That was the last time I washed Curdles! All these head injuries were starting to add up… hmmm.

The following school year, I told my mother I wanted to attend public high school. I'm not really sure why I wanted to switch away from the private Christian school, because in retrospect, I would be starting as a freshman in a public high school, again not knowing anyone. There may have been a few kids in the neighborhood that I had met that went to the public schools or maybe I was just a sucker for punishment. For some unknown reason, I was able to convince Mom to let me go to public school. After all, I had gone to public school from the first grade through seventh grade… I could handle this!

Public school turned out to be an absolute disaster. I started my ninth grade riding the bus to a high school I didn't know, with kids I didn't know, to begin classes with public school teachers who weren't necessarily mean, but they weren't Covenant teachers. I tried my hardest to fit in, but I just didn't. I did make a few friends, and one of them was actually a Christian. This was the only positive thing I had at this new school.

Because of the pain in my heart from the loss of my dad, my self-confidence had been destroyed, and the bullies had a field day with me. I remember sitting in class one day, and another boy had some candy. He saw me looking at the candy that he was sharing with his buddies. He asked if I wanted a piece, and for a moment, my eyes lit up as I thought he was actually being nice to me. When I held out my hand, he laughed, and looking around at his goon squad, he told me to lick the bottom of his shoe if I wanted to have some of the candy. I was crushed. I didn't understand what I had done to deserve this treatment.

Another time that I remember, I was walking down the hallway at school trying to get to my next class. A larger boy came up next to me and put his arm around me, walking with me. "Hey buddy," he said in an almost too friendly tone. I had a few classes with him and I knew he wasn't a nice person.

"Uh, hey?" I responded, suspicious of his intentions. We continued to walk and began to pass the door to the girls' restroom. Suddenly, the larger boy pushed me as hard as he could through the door to the bathroom so that I ended up inside! Maybe this bully was doing this because his friends were watching. Or maybe he was just doing it to be cruel and have something to brag about. This kind of bullying happened in many forms, almost on a daily basis. It made me dread going to school. And when you are fourteen years old, school is about all you have in your life, especially if you are not walking with the Lord.

I finally reached my breaking point after having been miserable for half the school year. I broke down and told my mother the hell I was going through. I begged to return to Covenant. How foolish I had been to want to change schools again! I was so relieved and thankful when Covenant agreed to allow me to come back midway through the year.

When I finally walked back into the doors at Covenant, I immediately felt like I had returned home. The bullying ended, but the damage had already been done. People wonder why children who are bullied have so many problems functioning.

When you don't feel like you matter, when you don't feel like you are worth anything, it tends to have an effect on your outlook on life. And when you don't know Jesus, the opinions of the world will have their way with your heart and mind. And on that thought, there is a world of difference between believing in God and having a relationship with Him. You see, you can believe all you want in something, but if it isn't true in your heart, it will never be more than a belief.

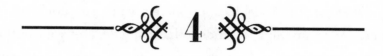

The Real World

I got my driver's license the day I turned sixteen. I had worked all summer doing landscaping work for a friend of Don and Sheila Richardson. I had saved up a few hundred dollars and I managed to find a car in the neighborhood that was for sale. My first car was a 1984 Ford Tempo, and it had actually been repainted at some point, so it looked very nice! My brother, Mike, was in town, so he and I took it for a test drive. As soon as we agreed on the price of $400 (all I had!), I eagerly thrust the wadded up cash into the owner's hands. I couldn't wait to get it home and clean it from the inside out!

What I would soon find out is that with a car comes a whole new level of freedom. Now that I could drive myself places, I stopped going to church and I started to do whatever I wanted. At this point in my life, I still believed in God, but I certainly was not at peace with Him and I had no real relationship with Him.

It was 1995 and I had just started my junior year in high school at Covenant. In order to pay for car insurance and gas, I got a job. I ended up with a job at Walmart in the automotive and hardware departments. I was cutting keys, mixing paint, selling hunting and fishing licenses, stocking shelves, and helping customers. I also learned how to run a cash register and a few other useful skills. While I was pretty good at mixing paint, I didn't know a lot about automotive. I thought I knew a lot because I had a car now... but it turns out the two don't always go hand in hand.

A lady came into Walmart one day as I was busily restocking the motor oil. She saw me working in my blue vest with a giant smiley face on the back and presumed that I was an expert mechanic. She proceeded to ask me how many quarts of oil she needed for her husband to change the engine oil in her car. With my superior knowledge base and years of experience, I asked her what kind of engine she had. I went on to tell her that if a car had a four-cylinder engine, it needed four quarts of oil. If a car had an eight-cylinder engine, it needed eight quarts of oil. I thought my logic was sound... it *sounded* like a good answer to me! That poor woman. I pray that her car was okay after my misguidance. An owner's manual is better than a sixteen-year-old kid at Walmart most days!

On the last day of my junior year in high school, I thought I would finish up the year with a way to be remembered. I had this Batman mask that was movie prop quality. I brought it with me to school that day, but I never had the guts to put it on. At the end of the day, I was sitting in the parking lot, getting ready to leave in my Ford Tempo (this was before I crashed it). I donned the Batman mask and was instantly transformed into the Dark Knight himself... driving a Ford Tempo. I backed out of my parking spot and drove through the lot with very little peripheral vision, drove out of the parking lot and down the street in front of the school. Like I had hoped, a few of my friends happened to see my car going by, only to see Batman himself behind the wheel. Mission accomplished.

That summer, while working at Walmart, I met a girl. I guess you could say she was my first girlfriend. I'll call her Melinda. Melinda came from a broken home and she was not a Christian. Her past was clouded with drugs and alcohol and sex and brokenness and darkness—and she was only fourteen when I met her. She had recently moved to Virginia from Florida. My standards weren't very high due to my low self-esteem, which had not yet recovered from my days being bullied. She took to me immediately, and so I jumped in with both feet. It didn't bother me that she was dysfunctional or even that she smoked cigarettes. I was just happy to be able to have someone who took a liking to me. At least I thought I was happy.

One night after working a shift at Walmart, I was driving home in my awesome car. I had bummed a cigarette from someone (yes, I picked up the habit for a couple of years, unfortunately) and when I finished smoking it, I flicked the butt out the window. I had the back windows rolled down partially, and in my rearview mirror, I thought I saw the still-lit cigarette fly back into the car behind me. I started to reach to the floorboard behind me with my right hand while bending over, all while still traveling about fifty-five miles per hour! I felt the road surface change, and I looked back up to see that my right front wheel had run off the roadway and was caught in a ditch. I saw the telephone pole only a second before I hit it. I had time to brace, and I screamed.

My 1984 Ford Tempo violently collided into the wooden telephone pole. The sound is all I remember, because my vision disappeared at that moment. The sickening sound of the smashed metal and breaking glass filled my ears. I didn't feel the bone in my left hand breaking as I bent the steering wheel while I braced myself. I lost consciousness for a moment, and when I came to, I was disoriented.

I knew I had struck the pole and I knew I was alive—but where was I? Was I now in the field on the side of the road? I could see headlights approaching off in the distance. As the headlights got closer and closer and became brighter and brighter, I heard the sound of screeching tires and another crash as the vehicle that was approaching sideswiped what was left of my car. It was then that I realized I was still on the road! After striking the pole, my car had spun around 180 degrees and bounced back into the roadway. The other car that hit me was just a glancing blow, thankfully.

Other than some seatbelt burn and the broken bone in the back of my left hand, I walked away from that crash. I thank God for protecting me. The passenger side front is what struck the pole, and as a result, the dashboard crushed in all the way to the passenger front seat. I am so thankful I did not have any passengers that night in late August. The moral of the story here? Smoking is bad for you! Oh, and the other car that hit me never stopped to say hi. Some people!

Of course, the Tempo was a total loss. So was the telephone pole—I received a bill from the power company a few weeks later for over $2500! The insurance took care of the bill and then dropped me like a hot rock. I did get another car within a few weeks. Now I had a 1986 Mercury Lynx with a five-speed manual transmission. This was the Mercury version of the Ford Escort, for all of you car enthusiasts! Learning to drive a five-speed with my left hand in a cast proved interesting and challenging. I wouldn't recommend it.

Melinda and her seventeen-year-old sister, who I'll call Lola, soon began to prove their true colors. Their alcoholic mother decided she was moving back to Florida, and so Lola and Melinda suddenly needed a place to stay, because at the ages of fourteen and seventeen, it made perfect sense for them not to go with their mother… right? My mother was still working night shift, and I somehow took advantage of her goodhearted kindness and convinced her to allow Melinda and Lola to move in with us. Once Melinda and Lola moved in, my mother told me I had to move out. It was immoral for me to live with Melinda because she was my girlfriend. Even though the circumstances were absolutely dysfunctional, I thought I was helping these "poor girls in need."

Who would open their home to a seventeen-year-old kid who needed a place to escape his own home due to his own foolishness? Don and Sheila Richardson. They allowed me to stay with them, and no doubt they saw the error of the situation, but they never gave me a hard time. They lovingly opened their home to me, and I moved in with them during the winter of my senior year in high school. Meanwhile, Sarah and my mother had to live with strangers, thanks to me.

It wasn't long before Melinda and I ended our meaningless relationship which we were convinced would last forever. It took a few months to get them out of my mother's home before they would both move back to Florida and out of my life. What a fool I was! Why was I drawn toward these broken, dark people? Why was I making decisions like this? It seemed like every choice I made was self-destructive and dysfunctional.

Walmart wasn't finished throwing trouble my way. My best friend at the time was also working at Walmart in the electronics department. I'll call him Charlie. Charlie got into trouble for stealing video games and a video game system from the store, and so he was charged with embezzlement. Charlie was still a juvenile when he got in trouble with the law, and so he was able to avoid becoming a convicted felon, but I was done with Walmart at that point.

While Charlie was going through this trial for his wrongdoings, I quit my job at Walmart. I wasn't going to work at a store that was charging my friend with a crime! As an employee, I had been given a Walmart Associate card which allowed me to get a small discount on store purchases as a benefit. As a way to demonstrate my anger with the situation, I decided to burn the associate card. This may not have been smart, but it was downright stupid to do under my desk while I was sitting in study hall!!

When the teacher detected the plastic burning smell, he thought it was an electrical problem and went to get the school maintenance man, Ricky. Ricky came into the room while I sat there in silence, regretting my foolish behavior. While Ricky and the teacher were searching for the source of the odor, another student who had seen my idiotic stunt decided that the charade had gone on long enough. The student piped up and told the teacher what had really happened. The teacher looked at me and said, "Jonathan, did you burn a credit card in here?" I stammered and tried to explain that it wasn't really a credit card... but it didn't matter. I got in-school suspension for a day for that. Looking back, I am lucky nothing more serious happened to the school!

Not all of my high school years were filled with dysfunction. I actually took a trip the summer before my senior year to Hungary. This was a mission trip to teach better English to Hungarian kids who knew some limited English already. I had to raise the money myself to cover airfare. I was the only boy that went on a trip with three girls and two female chaperones. It was actually fun, and I wish that I had a better memory of some of the experiences I had on that trip. Hungary is a beautiful country and was an introduction to a culture very different than what I was used to.

As "teachers," we actually had to come up with lesson plans to be able to have a curriculum to teach. This is how I discovered that I had absolutely no desire to be a teacher! The trip was bittersweet, however, as my grandmother (on my mother's side) died while I was away. After the "mission" part of the trip was over, we were able to spend some time sight-seeing in Europe, visiting places like Auschwitz in Poland and the city of Prague.

I know that I was very glad to graduate when the time came. After a summer of goofing off and hanging out with friends, I enrolled in the local community college with seventeen credit hours. A few electives, a couple of engineering classes, and a five credit math class—I had big aspirations. I was going to be an engineer like my dad before me. After all, it was in my blood, wasn't it?

About halfway through the first semester, I just didn't feel like going anymore. I had discovered that if I skipped a class or showed up late, there was no one to hold me accountable. No more detention, no more in-school suspension—I could do what I wanted! I wanted to have fun and I was done with this school nonsense. And so I did. And I failed every single class that I had enrolled for. Not the best start to my college career and a direct result of a depression I had been battling and a lack of motivation and maturity that I still carried.

After the stark reality of failing all of my classes set in, I was placed on academic probation with the college. After a while, I did start to slowly take a few classes at a time to get my GPA back up from a 0.0. I hopped from job to job, doing everything from selling cars to fixing mufflers to managing a florist (only lasted a week).

My mom had gotten out of working at the hospital and night shift and had become a partner in the ownership of a pediatric home health company. The company needed a delivery driver, and I got the job. It was during this time, in August of 1999, that I met the future Mrs. Jonathan Hickory.

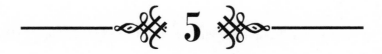

5

The Most Beautiful Girl

It was the worst first impression ever.

I came home from work, tired after a long day on the road, delivering medical supplies. I had been in the new job for a few months now and it sure beat working with hot exhaust pipes and dirty brake systems in a shop with no air conditioning. I was nineteen and I thought I knew it all. I had moved into an apartment about ten miles south of Charlottesville, Virginia. Pulling up to my brick apartment building in my black 1994 Acura Integra, I saw a little red Honda outside I didn't recognize. As I walked into my apartment, I saw that my roommate (and best friend), Kyle, had company. Inside I saw the most beautiful girl I had ever seen. Her name was Stacy and she was there visiting with her friend, Sarah.

Stacy was sitting in the sparsely furnished kitchen. She lit up the whole room—dingy linoleum, laminate backdrop, and all. She had piercing green eyes and long blonde hair that went all the way down her back. She was full of energy and joy. I had never set my eyes on a girl like this before and I was smitten.

There was something that drew me to her that I could not place. She had an air of pure confidence, but it wasn't the kind of confidence that was obnoxious or overly intimidating. This girl was different. I was definitely not looking for a relationship with a girl at that moment as I had recently gone through yet another unpleasant break-up with another broken young woman. Still, I wanted to impress this absolute fox!

I wasn't exactly dressed to impress. I must have changed after work, because I was wearing torn greasy blue jeans (with my kneecaps visible) and a *way* too tight white t-shirt. I strolled into the kitchen where Stacy was sitting at the beat-up wooden farm table and casually said hello, like I wasn't *dying* to meet her. I grabbed a beverage (possibly alcoholic) out of the fridge and lit up a cigarette. Not very classy. To this day, I am not sure why she ever gave me a chance. I believe I even offered her one of these possible alcoholic beverages (which she declined) to add to my attempted swagger.

I sat down across the table from this supermodel, and I remember she was looking through the yellow pages. You see, back in those days, we still had phone books. This was before smart phones, and we didn't even think to fire up the old Gateway desktop to connect via dialup with the 56K modem. Curious and attempting chivalry, I asked her what she was looking for.

She told me that she was looking for a restaurant so that she could take a friend of hers out to dinner. Being the money-conscious, almost twenty-year-old that I was, I asked Stacy what her budget was. She looked me directly in the eye and replied with what I perceived as an arrogant tone, "Oh, money is no object."

Well, hold the phone! She must come from money! I was immediately wondering (out loud) who this girl thought she was… seeing how I was a self-made man who worked hard for my money! This was the old me, quick to judge and inserting feet into my mouth. Stacy went on to explain that she meant that she didn't mind spending extra for this friend because it was a special occasion. Boy, did I feel dumb. I tried to play it off, but I felt like I had ruined any chance I had with this amazing, gorgeous beauty.

I thought about her for the next two weeks and even prayed to God that she was the one for me. I still believed in God, of course, but He and I weren't on the best terms. I still harbored anger toward the Lord after the loss of my father. This anger was also making appearances in the way I would react to things in my everyday life, from driving to phone conversations with irritated customers.

About two weeks later, a few of my friends and I went out to celebrate my birthday at the local Chili's. I could not believe my good fortune when Stacy showed up. I remember Stacy and I kept catching each other's glances, and for once, I wasn't too shy to hold her gaze for a few moments before looking away. We both knew there was something there. God made it easy for me, which is good because if it had been in my hands alone, it would have ended very badly. I got Stacy's phone number that night, along with a little note she wrote underneath of it: "Don't lose this." I still have that little slip of paper in my wallet, eighteen years later.

"I was, uh, wondering, if, uh, you would like to go out? I mean, sometime," I stammered through the question, which I had rehearsed so many times before I called her. I could picture Stacy rolling her eyes on the other end of the phone. I picked her up that weekend on a Saturday morning. We had planned to go for a hike to a nearby mountain trail called Old Rag. I must have spent forty-five minutes picking out my outfit the night before—the cleanest pair of trendy blue jeans I owned (that weren't very trendy), Timberland hiking boots, and a rugged looking, yet casual gray shirt.

My heart felt like it was going to beat out of my chest as I pulled into the driveway of Stacy's parents' house. The house was a small white early 1900s two-story with black shutters and a tin roof. A small concrete front porch led up to a solid white front door. The gravel in the driveway crunched under my feet as I nervously started walking up to the house. Just as I was about to reach the porch, I was intercepted by Stacy's father. *Oh crap.*

Lowell Badgley must have asked me seventy-five questions before allowing me into the house. As a matter of fact, I don't know if I ever made it into the house that day. I felt like I was being interviewed by the director of the FBI! Lowell wanted to know who this nineteen-year-old kid was that was trying to catch his daughter's eye.

Lowell is about as patriotic as they come. When I think of Lowell, "Stars and Stripes Forever" plays proudly in the background. Lowell did two tours in Vietnam in the navy. Lowell and every single male in his family made Eagle Scout. I'm pretty sure that if you failed to make Eagle Scout in the Badgley family, you might be banned for life. He and his wife, Dawn, were (and still are) the most active American Legion and American Legion Auxiliary members I have ever met.

During my interrogation—I mean, during our conversation—I talked about my job as a delivery driver (very impressive) and my college aspirations. I conveniently left out the part where I failed all my classes for lack of effort during my first year of college.

I tried to talk myself up the best I could, all the while trying to peer around Lowell to see if Stacy knew I was being grilled under the hot lamp just outside.

I was giving Lowell a hard time for probing for my life story (past and future) on that doorstep, but the truth is that if more fathers would take an interest in who their daughters were dating, the world would be a better place. I absolutely respected his protective nature and his genuine concern for his daughter, but this didn't change the amount of shaking my feet were doing in my boots.

Somehow I made it out of there alive with Stacy in the passenger seat. We hiked that mountain all day, and it was dark by the time we got back to the car. This marvelous girl was radiant inside *and* out. Stacy was raised in a Christian home. She wasn't full of brokenness, she didn't come from a dysfunctional family, and she was just too good to be true. We had a wonderful first date together, and I was sure I was absolutely in love. I even gave up cigarettes after that, because I knew she wasn't a fan. We continued to date for a little over a year and half before I asked her to marry me.

I wrote Lowell a letter requesting his permission to marry his only daughter. He asked me to meet with him regarding the matter, and one night, he and I had *the talk*. If I thought my nerves were shot before, I was prepared for the worst. Through God's grace, he and Dawn granted their blessing. It was the year 2001, and it would be another three and a half years before Stacy and I were married. Yes, it was a long engagement, but I had promised Lowell and Dawn that Stacy and I would not get married until she finished college.

Before we were married, I decided to pursue a career in Information Technology. I had started early with computers, dialing up to Prodigy Online at the age of nine in 1988 (thank you, Dad!). It was sad leaving the job with the home health company where I actually got to work with my mother, but I felt like things were moving too slowly for my patience, and I thought computers might have the answers to my ambition.

I worked for a while for a broadband company that sold something called SDSL to businesses. Just a quick explanation for the less technically minded: SDSL is an acronym for Synchronous Digital Subscriber Line (I totally wrote that from memory). Most homes have ADSL which is Asynchronous DSL. ADSL has a fast download speed and a slow upload speed. SDSL appealed to businesses because it had fast upload *and* download speeds.

I started my career with Broadslate Networks in 2001 and I worked my way into a promotion fairly quickly. I had great visions of working my way up into management, but the dot-com boom was hit hard by the terror attacks on September 11, 2001. By April of 2002, Broadslate Networks went Broadslate bankrupt, and I was laid off.

Unemployment is scary. I did become quite good at calling in and reporting all the jobs I had applied for that week so I could get my check from the unemployment office. I was thankful to have any income at all, even though the amount I was getting was a small fraction of what I was making. Not having a job and not being able to find another job was starting to toy with my self-esteem.

After five months of unemployment, I decided it was time to start exploring other options beyond the Information Technology world. IT jobs were scarce, and the people who were fortunate enough to still have a job working for a local government or some-thing more stable knew it. It was a bad time to be a nerd.

Everyone thinks about being a police officer at one point in their life, even if for a very brief moment. I had certainly thought about it before, and with all the craziness in the news at the time, I was really feeling like I wanted to do something to serve my country and protect my community. I knew a couple guys who worked for the local police department, so I put in an application. I was nervous, but in order to get to big places, to do good things, you have to take big first steps. Soon, I got a letter inviting me to the police applicant exams. Little did I know I was knocking on a door that would change my life forever.

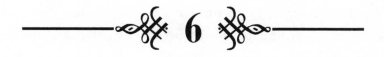

A Calling

I remember showing up *super* early for the police applicant test for the Albemarle County Police. It seemed like there were about one hundred people all crowded into one corner of the high school's cafeteria. It almost felt like the day I took my SAT tests in high school, bright fluorescent lighting casting down upon freshly sharpened number two pencils lying on the lunch tables. I assessed the competition, knowing that these were the people I was up against. Some of them looked the part of a cop with trim athletic physiques and military haircuts. Others looked like they had just rolled out of bed, disheveled and unkempt. The latter group were the ones I was glad to see, because I didn't feel like I belonged there myself. At twenty-two years old, I felt like I was physically fit enough to get through the agility test, but that didn't help much with my level of nervousness and anxiety.

All of the applicants were given a written test first. I remember it asked strange questions after giving you hypothetical scenarios. This was the part I thought was pretty easy. The test would give a description of a suspect in a robbery that had just occurred, and the bad guy was described as being a white male with brown hair and a red t-shirt, standing five feet, three inches tall. You were then told to pick the characteristic about the robber that would most easily make him identifiable if you were walking down the street. Hint: if you said it was brown hair, your calling may not be police work! There was also a vocabulary portion and a reading comprehension part of the test.

We were told that when we finished, we were to come back at 10:00 a.m. to check the list for our name to see if we had passed. If your name was on the list, you were to proceed to the gymnasium of the school for the physical agility test.

I came back and checked the list. It took me *forever* to find my name, but I finally found it. I had passed the test, thankfully. I made my way around the side of the brick-walled school to the gymnasium where the officers who were administering the physical agility test were waiting. It was intimidating to me; eight police officers all dressed in identical military looking clothing with blue BDU pants, tan polo shirts, and black boots. They weren't mean, but they weren't exactly officer friendly either. They barked instructions reminiscent of all those army movies I had seen with drill instructors in basic training.

Thankfully, I didn't have to go first. I watched other applicants running through the test, in dire fear that I was really going to foul things up when it came to be my turn. Others were stumbling and falling, running in the wrong direction, and collapsing. At times, it was like watching a team of five year olds trying to play a game of organized soccer.

The physical test was complicated, challenging, and nerve-wracking. A fresh applicant would start seated in a chair to simulate being seated in a police cruiser. After getting out of the chair, you had to climb over an eight-foot wooden obstacle. The eight-foot wall wasn't too bad because you could climb it like a ladder (provided you didn't break your ankle on the dismount). After the wall, you had to run a quarter of a mile in a figure eight crisscross pattern around little orange cones. It was confusing, but the officers administering the test helped you by pointing you where to go—you had to be able to comprehend instruction under pressure. The run was supposed to simulate a foot pursuit of a bad guy—a very confused bad guy. After the run, you were to jump a five foot simulated ditch (two sets of cones placed five feet apart). Some people's legs were so wiped after the run, they would fall on the simulated ditch jump.

The dummy pull was next. Applicants were instructed to pull a 150-pound dummy fifty feet to simulate rescuing someone who was unable to walk. At the end of all this, you drew your training gun from your holster (oh yes, you were doing all this wearing a duty belt and bullet proof vest) and pull the trigger five times with each hand. I'm getting tired just writing about it! They did not tell us what the passing time was, which just added to the stress.

After seeing several other people go through their agility test, it was finally my turn. My heartrate was up before I even left the chair at the beginning of the test. I somehow clambered over the eight-foot obstacle without falling on my face and remembered to pace myself during the run so I didn't run out of gas too soon. I bent over and hoisted the dead weight of the dummy, and about halfway through, the unthinkable happened as I lost one of my Nike running shoes! I just kept right on going. I wasn't about to stop and lose valuable time trying to get my shoe back on. I finished the test and I finished it with a passing time; luckily, having all the footwear you started with was not a passing requirement. I was told I would be contacted for an interview, and I left the gymnasium with my spirits high and exhilaration in the air!

The interview was conducted by a panel of police officers. Dressed as sharply as I knew how in my brand-new suit, I tried to appear confident and collected in the interview, making sure to make eye contact with everyone as I spoke. I remember sitting alone on one side of the long laminate topped table, looking across at four Albemarle officials. I guess Stacy's dad had prepared me well to answer questions under pressure, because I did well enough to move on to the background investigation.

I had to present college transcripts to the police department during this phase, and I made sure to write a letter explaining why I had dropped out of all of my classes my first semester in college. Thankfully, I had retaken many of those classes, and my GPA was at an acceptable level.

I also had to explain why my license had been suspended back when I was eighteen years old: I had been issued a ticket for having an expired safety inspection on my vehicle, and I decided that I wasn't going to pay it; after all, what could the government do to me? *Oh*. They can suspend your driver's license. I found out when I tore open the letter from the DMV one day. I immediately paid the court fines and had my driver's license reinstated the same day I received the letter. Lesson learned!

It was embarrassing to have to explain all my past mistakes and failures, but thankfully, my background investigator understood that young people don't always get it right the first time. I was recommended for hire. Everything was going my way, it seemed. Until it wasn't.

Looking back at who I was at that time in my life, I know that God's timing is perfect. I thought for sure I had the job. Visions of the police academy were filling my every daydream. Foolish pride and unfounded confidence can be dangerous and leave you with disappointment. I received a letter one day in July of 2002 from the police department. I fumbled with the envelope, trying to get it open as fast as I could. This was it! The moment I had been living for and the reason I caught every rerun of *COPS* I found on TV… until I actually started to read the letter.

My heart sank. The department had hired other applicants, and the letter was to thank me for my interest. I didn't understand! This was supposed to happen! "Not yet," God said.

Devastated, I continued my search for work. I thought about applying to another police department, but I really looked up to the officers of the Albemarle County Police.

I remember back when I was still in high school, I got a frantic call one night from my younger sister, Sarah, who was home by herself and said she had seen someone lurking in the woods outside of the house. She was probably fourteen or fifteen at the time. She had called 911 as well, so she really believed she saw someone. I raced home as fast as I could, determined to protect my sister. As I roared down the street toward the house, I remember seeing two blacked-out police cruisers parked well in advance of our driveway. These officers had the forethought to park further away and walk in so as not to alert the possible prowler. When I saw those police cars, any feelings of panic were immediately removed. Knowing that these guys were here made me feel safe. I respected that the officers took the report seriously, even though some might have thought my sister was imagining things. The two officers checked the area for a long time before saying they didn't see anyone, but asked us to call back if we saw anything else. This respect for the county police would always remain steadfast in my mind.

In August of 2002, I was able to find a job working in Information Technology support as a contract employee at GE Fanuc in Charlottesville. The pay wasn't bad, but there were no benefits included. I met some wonderful people there and often think back with good thoughts of the year I worked at GE, fixing computers and sharpening my knowledge of technology.

I continued to work at my goal of becoming a police officer, determined to prove myself worthy of hiring. A friend of mine who had served with the Albemarle County Sheriff's Office (different than the police department) recommended that I join the Sheriff's Reserve Division. This seemed like a good move as I could show that I was willing to volunteer to do police work, and perhaps it would help build my resume toward the direction of a police job. I signed up right away.

The Sheriff's Office Reserve Division taught me how to wear the police uniform and taught me how to perform some of the basic skills, like how to run a metal detector at the courthouse. I even got to help a full-time deputy with a prisoner transport from the local jail to a hospital over an hour away. It was my first time riding in a police car (that's a good thing) and my first time inside a jail (also a good thing). I remember the heavy metal green door of the jail slamming shut after the deputy and I came inside. The prisoner, dressed in a black and white striped jail uniform, seemed annoyed that we were making him put on leg shackles in addition to handcuffs for the trip. I felt nervous with a handcuffed criminal riding behind me, despite the loaded semiautomatic pistol in the holster on my side.

On the way, we came up on a pickup truck pulling a boat on the side of Interstate 81 in Augusta County. This normally wouldn't have been very exciting, except the boat was completely on fire! There wasn't much we could do beyond blocking traffic in the right lane and, of course, ensuring the safety of the motorists—but I was hooked! This was just a taste of what police officers deal with, and I was ready for more.

The timing was finally right. I was invited back to go through the hiring process with the Albemarle County Police a second time in 2003. This time, there were less than fifteen people taking the written test. I looked around and remember seeing a young man who had gone to high school with me named David. This time, I wasn't quite as nervous, and seeing an old friend helped. David would end up being hired a few years later.

This time, I didn't lose my shoe as I was sure to tie it extra tight, even double tie it. This time, the letter in the mail said something very different. "The Albemarle County Police Department is pleased to provide you with a conditional offer of employment," I read the professionally prepared stationery. The feeling of exhilaration had returned, and I was on top of the world! It had been one year and one month since I was turned down. I never thought at the time that God was involved, but now I know His timing was perfect as it always is.

To Protect and Serve

God was blessing me, despite my lack of a relationship with Him. I was about to start an exciting new job, I was to be married in less than a year to a sweet amazing woman, and I was healthy. Still, I tried not to think about the loss of my father. If I was alone at night watching TV or a movie and there was a scene showing a father and son in a bonding loving moment, I would cry. My anger issues did not surface quite as often as they used to when I was a teenager, but they were definitely still there.

One summer, while Stacy and I were engaged to be married, she was working at a Christian summer camp close to Richmond, Virginia. She went to close the door on her accidentally custom painted John Deere green (a story for another time) 1983 Mercury Zephyr after parking it and somehow her engagement ring diamond setting became caught in the door. The diamond itself went flying into the gravel as the prongs on the setting were smashed. Stacy began crying uncontrollably, she would tell me later. Stacy was not crying because she hurt her finger. After frantically searching for the diamond for several minutes, another camp counselor amazingly found the gem. When Stacy told me about it, she told me that she was crying because she was scared. She was so sure that I would be extremely angry with her for losing the diamond. This is the reality of who I was. It made me very sad to hear that my wife-to-be was scared of my anger problem.

In my heart, my anger had begun to grow at the moment I found out my father was going to die. Through the years of growing up and becoming a young man, this anger only burned hotter. I was angry with myself for not being a better son. I was angry with God for taking my dad away from me. I felt like everyone else was flourishing in life while I was struggling. When you are angry with yourself, angry at God, and angry at the world, darkness is given an open invitation to destroy your heart.

After Stacy and I started dating, she and I began to attend church together. We started to attend a tiny little church in Schuyler, Virginia, called New Faith United Methodist. Just up the street from the church was the site of Ike Godesy's General Store made famous by Schuyler resident Earl Hamner Jr. through *The Waltons*, a TV show. The church must have been one hundred years old. It was a charming little country church, painted white and complete with a church bell and a steeple.

New Faith Church was close to where Stacy's parents lived, and the church had a Virginia State Trooper as their pastor, which furthered my interest in becoming a police officer. Although the average age of the people in attendance was about three times my own, and the average attendance was less than twenty-five people, Stacy and I enjoyed going together. My dormant faith was slowly being nudged.

Although I thought I had Jesus in my heart, as soon as I walked out of the church, He was forgotten and not thought of again. I was doing just fine without God in my day-to-day life, and so I placed Him in the back of my heart.

I started the police academy in late August 2003. The academy that I attended served as an academy for multiple police and sheriff agencies in Virginia and was almost an hour's commute from where I lived in Charlottesville. Thankfully, the academy provided small dorm rooms where police recruits could stay, so I did not have to make the commute every day. The academy was a modern looking brick building nestled between sprawling corn fields and a community college in Virginia's Shenandoah Valley.

On the very first day, I remember being lined up with my back pressed against the pristine white painted cinder block wall, my bag neatly propped at my feet. All the other new students began showing up and did the same. I was excited but I was shaking like a leaf. I tried not to let the other students see that I was nervous, but I knew they could see it. In marched the police academy training coordinator, barking at everyone, "Get off my wall!" We all shot up off the wall and snapped to attention. This was day one!

The next fifteen weeks of training were packed with studying, tests, pushups, running, and practical training exercises. Cops like to joke about the reason they became officers, to drive fast, and shoot guns. Fortunately for American citizens, the basic police academy covers a lot more than that. A few of the things I learned in the academy: how to make traffic stops, how to correctly handcuff people, defensive tactics, safely shooting a pistol, emergency and pursuit vehicle operation, arduous amounts of law, search and seizure, crime

scene processing, motor vehicle crash investigation, DUI investigation, domestic violence, and much more. I was full of energy and
passion for every topic I learned about. Now that I was pretty sure I
knew so much, I was eager to get out there and apply it.

In November of 2003, I graduated from the police academy and
was sworn in as an officer by the clerk of the court. My field training
experience began about a week later. After completing the academy,
new officers have to complete a twelve-week on-the-job training with
a field training officer (FTO). My FTO was Officer Steve Watson.
Once I finally hit the streets with my FTO, I found out how little I
actually knew about the job. I was assigned to midnight shift, working from 11:30 at night until 8:30 a.m.

One of the first traumatic calls I remember being dispatched to
was for an assist of the rescue squad. A man had received a phone call
from his elderly neighbor in the townhome next door. The elderly
woman said, "I need help," and then the phone went dead. It was
3:00 a.m., and that was all we had to go on. I frantically looked at the
map book, trying to determine where the address was and how to get
there from my location. We didn't have a GPS as it was not generally
accepted at the time; GPS navigation had only recently come available to the public three years prior.

I found what I thought was the best route to the call and got
there as fast as I could. It was a cold night in early December. Steve
and I knocked on the door of the elderly woman's home and received
no response. My FTO peered in through the Sidelite window panes
next to the front door, and said, "I can see her feet, she's lying on the
floor."

I started to panic. We had to get in to help this woman now! The door was locked. I pulled out my expandable baton and began to strike the window panes in an attempt to break the glass. It didn't work! The lady must have had some sort of security glass, because it wasn't budging, not even a crack. As I wailed on the glass, Steve had the ingenuity to run around the back of the house and found a window that was unlocked. Steve cut the screen as quickly as he could and ran to the front door to let the rescue squad in. Thank God! Now we could help this poor woman!

The rescue squad members burst into the home, quickly attending to the elderly woman lying on her back on the floor. The victim was a female in her seventies with white hair and wearing a white nightgown. She was warm to the touch but she had no pulse.

I watched helplessly as a team of medics pumped on the frail woman's chest. Seconds turned into minutes as they did everything they could to save her. Watching CPR in progress is like watching a dance of desperation, but there is no beauty in the dance. The naive hope that this lady would survive began to fade with every passing moment of unresponsiveness. That hope was destroyed completely as the senior medic looked at his watch, calling the time of death. And then, just like that, the team of rescue personnel suddenly ended their lifesaving attempts.

A silent empty house and the motionless lifeless shell of an elderly woman lay before me. It was now up to me to deal with the scene. I never thought that I would find myself in this situation as a police officer. These are the things you just don't think about when you glorify the image of being a hero police officer in your mind. I was thankful for the guidance of my field training officer as he instructed me how to obtain permission to have the body removed by a funeral home.

After the shift, I couldn't get the image of this woman's face out of my mind. Her lifeless, void eyes staring back at me. It wasn't a violent death, but it was the first dead body I had seen. My father's memorial service had no casket, no body. My grandmother died while I was on a mission trip out of the country, my grandfather died when I was twenty years old, and I never saw their bodies either. The thoughts of the death bothered and haunted me. Of course, I didn't tell anyone, because I was supposed to be tough. I swallowed the images of the scene and the uncertainty and sad feelings and I moved on. Because that's what us guys do, right?

It wasn't long after that night that I found myself pointing my gun at someone for the first time. This was not a moment I was looking forward to and it absolutely terrified me. My training officer and I had responded to a report of someone firing rifles in the early morning hours, around one o'clock. I remember being very glad that I had my training officer with me, because I didn't want to go into this situation alone. As we approached the address in the still of the winter night, we turned off the headlights on the cruiser and walked the rest of the way on foot. In police work, you never know what to expect and you cannot be too careful when you are dealing with people with firearms.

To be safe, we waited for another officer to arrive before walking in. The frozen brittle dirt road made a stealthy approach challenging as we did our best to walk in silently. We maneuvered the maze of shadows cast by the pale moonlight through the overlying tree branches. Upon reaching the driveway, we carefully began our approach to the house. Dimly lit windows gave an eerie glow from the one story structure, and I could feel the vibration of the bass from blaring loud music.

Out of the corner of my eye, I detected movement. Two white males had appeared from the side door of the small white house and both were carrying guns. I don't remember drawing my own gun, but suddenly there it was in my hands with the barrel leveled on these two armed men. I began screaming over and over in vain, "*Drop the gun! Police! Drop the gun!*"

As I stood there attempting to get these two men to comply with my commands, I mentally took in their descriptions. The exterior lighting was poor, but I could see the guns clearly. Both men appeared to be in their twenties and they were both holding semi-automatic rifles. One of the guns looked like an AK-47, and the other appeared to be some sort of SKS Soviet military rifle. The thoughts raced through my mind, wondering if I was going to make it through this alive. I was definitely outgunned and I was also downhill from the suspects, giving me the tactical disadvantage. At some point, I ended up on my belly, lying face down so that I would be harder to hit.

As my training officer and I continued to command the men to drop their weapons, the anxiety level increased when both suspects completely ignored the orders. One of the two suspects raised his rifle and fired off a shot, not in our direction, but it still made my insides twist in fear. As I continued to yell over and over at the top of my lungs, the suspect who was closer to me suddenly turned in my direction, sweeping his rifle around until it pointed toward me for a moment.

My finger moved instinctively to the trigger of my police issued handgun, preparing to fire. Although the moment seemed to last an eternity, a split-second later, the male turned the rifle back toward the house and proceeded to walk inside. The other male followed. I was left lying there on the icy ground, dumbfounded. The clear crisp air was clouded by my breath vapors as I tried to process what had just happened. I had only been at this for a few weeks and I couldn't believe what I was experiencing.

We waited. And we waited. About an hour later, I had lost most of the feeling in my fingers, but I still had my pistol aimed and ready, the night sights on the top of my weapon glowing against the darkness. As my FTO and I lay with our eyes trained on the house, the booming bass finally stopped. The lights in the house started to go off one by one. The two suspects came out of the house again. This time (thank God) I did not see any rifles. A second later, we were advancing on the suspects, screaming, *"Police! Get your hands up! Keep your hands where we can see them!"*

The two suspects complied this time. It was as if they never knew we were there before. The other officer and I kept our guns pointed at the bad guys while my training officer placed them each in handcuffs. *It was over.* As it turned out, they were both *extremely* drunk and had no clue that the police were there the whole time. They claimed to never have heard us yelling at them and never saw us, their senses apparently clouded by their inebriation and the loud music emanating from the house. I remember being so *angry* with these two! Of course, I knew better than to act on my feelings, but the danger they had placed me in had my blood boiling. My training officer and I were able to charge both of them with being drunk in public and reckless handling of a firearm. They got a free stay in jail that night for their behavior.

My *very first* traffic stop turned into a Driving Under the Influence (DUI) arrest. It was almost Christmas, it was just after two o'clock in the morning, and it had just begun to snow. Beautiful heavy flakes were rapidly coating the pavement in a soft white carpet. My head on a swivel, I suspected every vehicle around me to be filled with lawbreakers and evildoers. That's when I noticed the Nissan Pathfinder in front of me as it began to drift into the other lane as it traveled over fifteen miles above the speed limit.

My voice shook as I called in the traffic stop. I messed up the order of how I was supposed to call it in and I was having trouble reading the license plate through the thick snowflakes. My nerves were completely shot and the adrenaline flow quickened my heart rate and my breathing. Somehow I was able to control the police car enough to maneuver behind the Nissan as my FTO turned on the blue flashing lights to initiate the stop. I reached over for the faded spotlight and flicked it on, shining its tired beam on the driver.

I cautiously approached the car. I gripped my brand new Maglite in my left hand, making sure to have my weapon hand free in case I needed to quickly draw my gun. I half expected the driver to jump out with a machine gun and start blasting me since I had been trained in the academy that every car I stopped had the potential to kill. As I walked up and began illuminating the interior of the SUV, I could see the driver appeared to be staring ahead in a trance-like state.

The window whirred as it opened slowly, and I asked the man for his driver's license. *At least I got that part right*, I thought. As the driver fumbled through his wallet, I got my first whiff of the odor.

The pungent sweet smell of an alcoholic beverage is very hard to hide and very easily identified, especially after being bottled up in a warm car with the windows up. I tried not to let on that I smelled booze and thanked the man for his license once he finally was able to find it. I knew what was coming next. I fished the card with the standardized field sobriety tests on it out of my pocket, dropping it at least once as I struggled to balance it in my hands with my flashlight, my notepad, and my pen.

Back in the academy, I had been given training on how to do these tests. We even had volunteers come in and get drunk for the police recruits so we could run them through the sobriety tests. But it's so different in the real world. It wasn't snowing in the gymnasium where we held the practice tests. You also didn't need a flashlight. The driver had admitted to me to having "a couple beers." Over the years, I have learned that this is the standard answer for a drunk driver—never just one, never six or seven, always "a couple."

As the driver stepped out, he towered over me at over six feet, five inches tall. At just under six feet myself, I suddenly felt threatened by his size. Despite being intoxicated, however, this guy was actually really nice. He agreed to perform the sobriety tests, and even though it was my first time giving them in a real scenario, I could tell he was not doing well.

As I told him to turn around and put his hands behind his back, I thought for sure I was going to have to fight him. To my (pleasant) surprise, he was fully compliant and stood there quietly as I fumbled with the cold steel handcuffs. Later, while we were at the jail, the arrestee began to cry as he began realizing the reality of the situation. Unable to even wipe his own tears, I felt sorry for this man. I didn't feel bad for arresting him, because I knew it had to be done to keep the streets safe, but I had compassion for him as I could see that the drinking and driving were a window into obvious deeper problems in his life.

As I was exposed to all these experiences, which I had never seen or done before, I was quickly beginning to realize how crazy and unsettled a place the world could be. Sure, you hear about the arrests, the violence, robberies, and unrest on the news. But when *you* are the one who actually has to deal with these situations, it opens your eyes to a different side of humanity than you are used to seeing. As a police officer, you don't often meet people on their best day. Whether you are trying not to lose your lunch because of all the blood and brain matter at the violent suicide scene or whether you are telling a mother that her son was just killed in a horrid car crash, you are constantly witnessing (first-hand) some of the darkest moments in people's lives and in this fallen world. If you do not have a real relationship with God, these dark moments and dark times begin to darken your soul.

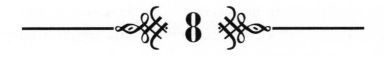

Tough It Out

Stacy had graduated from college, and we were so excited to begin our lives together. On Memorial Day weekend 2004, she and I were married on an unseasonably warm day at a local vineyard. We were full of youth, joy, hope, and love. All we needed was each other and we felt like we could take on the world. We spent our wedding day surrounded by our closest friends and family and we were happy. God had certainly blessed me with this amazing, loving, sweet, beautiful woman.

I had finally completed my field training program with the police department in the spring of 2004, just a couple of months before getting married. I felt so incredibly accomplished and I was definitely ready to be out on my own as a new police officer. I was ready to be the best officer I could be.

Before I finished my twelve weeks of field training, I was told by my field training officer that I had one thing I needed to work on—I needed to watch the way I spoke to people. My FTO had noticed that during my field training, as I had encountered a few people, my tone sounded very angry and even condescending. My anger was showing its ugly head once again. I became more conscious of how I spoke to people I came into contact with and began to be more careful, but I was still filled with rage inside. Police work is not a good profession to be angry or to take your interactions personally.

As the months and then years went by, the things I was experiencing in police work weren't getting any easier. I began to live and breathe my job, being a cop on *and* off duty. I loved the job and I felt like I was making a difference, but the repeated exposure to trauma, conflict, dysfunction, and brokenness soon started to wear on me. Without a strong faith in God, I could only turn to other officers and my wife to cope with the fatigue of my soul. Other officers seemed to carry the mentality "tough it out, suck it up." I didn't feel like Stacy would understand what I was going through and seeing as a cop. I did not want to be seen as weak by my wife or anyone else. I began to feel alone and hopeless.

I have heard that you should never take your work home with you, especially police work. You don't want to try to control your wife and family like you have to control situations as a police officer. Unfortunately, since I was living and breathing the cop life, this was easier said than done. I often would lash out and be verbally abusive to my loving wife, who of course did not deserve such treatment.

I remember one time I had not cut the grass (in way too long) at our little blue house that we began renting after we were married. Maybe I was busy or maybe I was feeling lazy; I'm not sure why I let the grass get so long. It was a hot summer evening, and Stacy was so upset that the grass needed to be mowed, she got the push mower out and began to trudge through that thick grass herself. I was so angry at the time that I just watched her struggle with the mower, her determined spirit unwavering. She made it a few passes on the lawn, and I could hear the groaning engine of the lawn mower as it fought the jungle of grass.

The mower finally stalled, and Stacy took it as a good time to rehydrate. Sweaty and breathing hard from the workout, Stacy walked in from where she was pushing the mower and asked if I would get her a glass of water. My anger still burned. I refused to get my wife a glass of water, making sure to tell her that since I didn't want her to mow the grass in the first place (it was *my* job, even though I had procrastinated). I would not help her. What a fool I was—an angry, self-righteous fool. To this day, I am ashamed of my behavior, but this is just a small glimpse into the person I was.

The anger I felt and the stress of police work soon led me to turn to alcohol as a way of to cope. Drinking beer and wine became a part of my normal routine after work. I began to look forward to that numbing feeling that I got when I drank—it was a way for me to forget about the reality of the torn world I lived in, a way to drown the memory of the death of my father, and a way to ease the edge of the violence and death I was beginning to see so much of. On the outside, everything seemed to be going well for me. On the inside, my heart ached with pain and depression. I was miserable and filled with emptiness.

One day, while I was working, another officer offered to let me try smokeless tobacco or "dip." The tobacco comes in a small can that looks like a hockey puck. You take a pinch of the tobacco out of the can and you place it between your gums and your cheek. I had tried "dip" when I was younger, but it always made me sick. This time, I was offered an apple flavored tobacco that almost tasted like candy. It didn't take long before I was using "dip" on my own, and it became a habit that I would not quit for twelve more years. I easily justified the habit since almost every cop I knew was doing it, and it seemed to help me cope with the stress of the job. Because she disapproved, I hid the habit (the best I could) from Stacy.

Stacy and I eventually bought our first house, a charming gray ranch on two acres. We were blessed with the birth of our daughter, Ana Grace, in October of 2009. This was my introduction to fatherhood. I wanted to be the best father in the world for my daughter since I lost my father when I was a child. I tried to ease up on my drinking, but I could not quit. I denied it, but I was becoming an alcoholic. I became irritable (even more so than usual) and had difficulty sleeping without alcohol. And so the drinking continued. I even began to hide the alcohol from my wife, going out of my way to buy extra liquor or wine that Stacy never knew I had. It would appear to her that I had only drank a couple of beers, but in reality, I would drink the beer and also drink large amounts of liquor. The problem was getting worse.

The effects of alcohol are horrid. Most everyone knows what it is like to be "hung over" the next day after drinking. Imagine being trapped into drinking every day and feeling hung over every day as well. If I did not drink, my body would physically begin to itch and twitch. I was constantly in a state of irritability, because my body was going through withdrawals the moment I was not feeding my addiction. My family suffered. I suffered. I felt there was no escape and I tried to normalize my behavior. When other cops talked about drinking, I would get on board with the conversation and it would make me feel like it was okay to have a drinking habit.

Because I was hiding my drinking habit from Stacy, I would often wait until she went to bed before drinking heavily. Often going to bed between 3:00 a.m. and 5:00 a.m., I would sleep life away the next day until it was time to get ready for work. I had no interests outside of working and drinking, not even the gift of my beautiful family. It was a miserable existence, a vicious cycle.

After about four years as a patrol officer, I was accepted into a position with the department's Traffic Safety Unit. I had a passion for DUI enforcement and traffic enforcement and often led my shift in traffic tickets. Being young and full of enthusiasm, I stopped as many cars as I could and tried to write at least two tickets per shift. As a result, I was awarded a drunk driving enforcement award from the local chapter of Mothers Against Drunk Driving. I received these awards three years in a row. To me, it was a big deal to receive the awards. My wife and I were invited to dine with the chief of police at a special banquet for award recipients. Face time with the chief and a free meal were both good things for a young cop trying to make a name for himself.

As a member of the Traffic Safety Unit, I basically had two jobs—write tickets (*lots* of tickets) and investigate motor vehicle crashes. I even trained to be a motorcycle officer, which I thought was really cool. I loved to ride motorcycles, and now I could ride one *and* get paid for it.

Investigating and reconstructing motor vehicle crashes involving death was the only part of being a Traffic Safety Officer that I dreaded. Even after a few years as a police officer, I still had a real problem dealing with death. I hoped that moving to the traffic safety position would get me away from the death scenes on the street. After transferring to the unit, I even cut back on my drinking for a while. It wasn't long before I had to work my first fatality crash.

I remember being called out from home for the first time as a fatal crash investigator. It was a hot and humid night in mid-July, and it was just after midnight. On the road leading to Thomas Jefferson's Monticello, two cars filled with young males had been racing each other. One of the cars lost control coming around a curve and slid off of the road, crashing roof first into a tree. When I got the call, I was nervous and excited at the same time. Having recently completed a two-week long training course on crash reconstruction and investigation, I was ready to apply what I had learned. I got ready as quickly as I could and raced off toward the scene.

When I arrived at the scene of the crash, the blinding brilliance of emergency lights lit up the night. Fire trucks, ambulances, and police cars fought for space on the two-lane pavement. I got as close to the crash as I could and threw the gear selector on my unmarked police car into park. I could see the car, a late nineties model black Acura Integra, exactly like the kind of car I used to drive. Fresh tire marks led up to the mangled metal heap before me. The Integra had impacted a tree with its roofline, causing the roof to crush into the skull of the defenseless passenger. The deceased passenger was still in the front seat. I didn't want to look, but it was my job to look. I crept closer to the still figure of the passenger, nervously approaching the broken body. I stared into the eyes of the dead young man, and his lifeless eyes stared beyond mine. *This never gets easier for me*, I thought. When you are already in the dark, death only leads to more darkness.

Although the carnage before me disturbed my soul, I put on my game face and went to work. I busied myself with taking pictures and measurements and tried not to think about the gruesome reality of the sweet sticky smell of death coming from that car.

The driver of the car was another young man, only eighteen years old. I'll call him Aaron. Aaron was just beginning his adult life and was attending the local community college. He had been hanging out with his friends, had a few beers, and driven foolishly and recklessly. For this decision, Aaron would now be a convicted felon for the rest of his life, would also be spending some time in prison, and had to cope with what he had done.

I thought how easily this could have been me in Aaron's shoes. Fueled by my unresolved deep anger at life, my own driving behavior when I was younger was extremely dangerous and risky. Racing, passing on double yellow lines, and excessive speed defined my driving. Although I got a ticket here and there, I got away with a lot more than I should have.

I remember a few of my friends and I used to take our cars after school and try to "catch air" while jumping a blind hill that crossed some old railroad tracks. This was right in the middle of a residential neighborhood, and we had no way of knowing if a child was on the other side of the blind hill. I shudder to think what could have happened as a result of my stupidity and foolishness. Zipping around back country roads at speeds over eighty miles per hour, it's only by the grace of God that I am still alive. After several years of investigating crashes involving death, I have been constantly reminded of how irresponsible I was.

When I was around eighteen years old, I drove a lifted pickup truck for a while. I was trying to impress one of my many broken girlfriends, and she liked the truck. It was a blue 1988 Toyota with a six-inch suspension lift and thirty-five-inch tall mud tires. I even put a roll bar in the bed with ridiculous spotlights mounted on top.

One day, I went to pick up my mother from her office in that jacked-up truck. I was taking her out to lunch. I was so full of rage that day, I started to drive foolishly and recklessly. I was not angry with my mother, just the world, as usual. Spinning my wheels, speeding, and challenging other drivers, I was scaring my mother to death. She voiced her concerns and pleaded with me to stop driving in this manner, but I only ignored her. Finally, my poor mother demanded that I drop her back off at her office. This made me even more enraged, because now I was mad at myself for being such a fool. I dropped her off, and as soon as she had closed her door, I sped off through the parking lot—a ridiculous boy filled with anger and hatred for the world in his ridiculous truck.

As soon as I got home that night, after hours on the scene, I began to drink. I could not get the bottles open fast enough. I wanted to forget everything I had just seen, and soon I was slipping into the numbness I knew so well. I wanted to be better than this, I didn't want to depend on alcohol—but I felt that it was the only thing that could erase the trauma I had been exposed to.

I somehow continued to function as an alcoholic. My family suffered as I continued to drink heavily every night. I justified the drinking with the stress of the job. Other officers often spoke of how they could not wait to get home to drink beer. This helped with the secret alcoholism that I was constantly ashamed of as I believed that all officers drank to medicate their sorrows.

Yes, I was doing just fine. Married, a beautiful healthy daughter, a position in a specialized unit, and I even got to ride a motorcycle at work! To others, I was a success. To others, I wore my mask well, hiding my torment behind it. I smiled for pictures, putting on a facade of happiness.

Inside, my heart was getting dark and cold. My heart of flesh was turning to a heart of stone. The more I drank, the less emotion I felt about these violent death scenes… and I liked that. The more I drank, the further I withdrew from any kind of relationship with God. I yelled at my wife and I screamed at my daughter. Angry outbursts became a daily activity for me. I was dying inside and my life was beginning to falling apart.

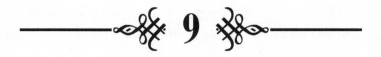

Daniel

I remember the day like it was yesterday. It was autumn of 2010, and I had been a crash reconstruction officer for about a year. I continued to function in a state of misery and alcohol addiction and abuse. I worked evening hours, escaping the responsibility of my family five days a week. As soon as I was able to every night, the drinking would begin. I would sleep into the late hours of the day, whenever I could, and tried to forget how much I hated myself.

I had just walked out of traffic court and was hoping to get a late lunch when I heard the call. Officers were responding for a car versus motorcycle crash, and the motorcyclist was down. No other crash reconstruction officers were available, and this crash sounded pretty bad. I let the dispatcher know that I was clear from court and that I would be on the way to the crash.

It was a clear, sunny, rather pleasant day in early October. The wailing of my siren screamed for people to get out of my way, but it seemed that no one saw or heard my frantic effort behind them. I felt like an invisible ghost car trying to make my way through the endless sea of traffic ahead of me. After what felt like an eternity of running code (blue lights and siren), I arrived on the scene.

As I maneuvered my way through the maze of emergency vehicles and police tape, stepping over the debris field of vehicle parts, I started taking the scene in around me as I snapped pictures with my digital camera. This was a relatively straight stretch of a rural two-lane road. A heavily damaged, cherry red colored Ford Taurus station wagon sat half on, half off of the pavement, facing the wrong direction. The obliterated remains of a black sport motorcycle had smashed through the wooden privacy fence of a nearby home. The motorcycle was completely destroyed. A green landscaping tarp covered up something on the side of the road.

A volunteer firefighter walked up to me, holding a driver's license. "This came out of his wallet, which we found over there," the firefighter gestured to his right.

"Whose wallet?" I asked.

"The guy on the motorcycle," the firefighter replied plainly.

"Is he being transported?" I asked the firefighter.

"No, he's dead. He's under that tarp over there." Again the firefighter gestured, with little emotion.

Great, another death scene. My mind started racing with apprehension. I looked down at the driver's license I held in my hand. I hadn't really looked at it until now. My eyes fell upon the name and the picture at the same instant. The license began to shake as I felt my hand trembling. In that instant, my heart sank. *Daniel!* I could not believe it. This couldn't be real. It couldn't be happening.

When I was in my senior year in high school, we had a new kid show up. Our entire senior class was only about forty kids, so new people were not only rare but stood out. Daniel, or Dan as we called him, was very different. With his long blonde hair in a pony-tail and his black leather motorcycle jacket, he hardly fit the mold of your typical Covenant School student. Dan had that tough guy exterior and he mostly kept to himself. I didn't know what Dan's story was, why he suddenly showed up in a private Christian school in his senior year, but that was part of the mystery… part of the bad boy image, I suppose.

In reality, Dan was a very genuine, kind, and noble young man. He liked motorcycles and actually rode one. To me, as a somewhat nerdy sixteen-year-old, this put Dan at *super* bad to the bone status.

Fast forward thirteen years to this dark day I was living in the moment of. Dan had just eaten lunch with his new bride and he was enjoying the beautiful weather on his motorcycle, traveling back to the vineyard where he was a rising, award-winning young vintner. As he rode along, little did he know that this would be the last time he saw his wife. Little did he know that this would be the last time he would ride a motorcycle. Little did he know that his life was about to end.

As Dan rode along behind a line of traffic, the cherry red Ford station wagon approached from the opposite direction at a high rate of speed. The driver of the Ford suddenly veered off the side of the road and overcorrected, causing the Ford to spin counter-clockwise while it slid sideways, taking up the entire roadway as it slid. There was nothing Dan could do.

The fluid dump at the time of impact showed that Dan had tried to move to the right, trying to avoid being struck by the car, but there was nowhere to go. The car struck him at a speed I would later calculate to be in excess of sixty-five miles per hour, although the speed limit was forty-five. Dan's body went flying up into the air and landed nearby on the side of the road. I have no doubt in my mind that Dan died instantly. A young man with a bright and promising future filled with love, robbed of his life in a split-second.

I tried to put the horrid thoughts of reality out of my mind. I had work to do. I was going to get justice for Dan. I went over to verify the identity of the motorcyclist, carefully and dreadfully pulling the lime green tarp away from his face. My fear was confirmed in that moment as I looked down at Dan's face. Covered in blood, my fallen comrade lay before me. I was in disbelief and I was angry. The rescue squad had removed his helmet to try to save him, but he was already gone. His body was broken and his clothes were torn, all dignity removed.

I remember finding the empty bottle of Jack Daniels whiskey in the cherry red Ford station wagon. The receipt was still in the bag with the empty bottle, complete with a time stamp. The driver had purchased the pint of whiskey only ten minutes after the liquor store opened earlier that morning. In less than three hours, the driver had consumed the entire pint of whiskey and was driving in an extremely inebriated state. His decision to drive under the influence had directly caused the death of Dan.

Armed with this evidence, other assisting officers were able to obtain a search warrant for the drunk driver's blood. I stayed on scene for hours. It was dark when I finally did finish my work for the day, but I didn't mind.

The next day, I reached out to Dan's family. I was able to make arrangements to bring some of Dan's belongings out to his wife and parents. I gathered Dan's backpack and his motorcycle helmet and began the drive out to meet his family.

When I arrived, I felt like I did not belong. It was just after dusk on a Tuesday night. Dan's family was trying to mourn the loss of this young son and husband. As I walked through the door of the small yellow house, carrying the personal effects of their loved one, I suddenly felt very much out of place—like I had somehow violated this sacred gathering with my presence. All of the family members sat quietly around the living room, patiently awaiting my arrival.

I was immediately welcomed by the family with warmth and appreciation. My anxiety slowly began to slip away as I realized that these were just people; people who were greatly hurting. Tom, Dan's stepfather, acted as a sort of liaison for the family and introduced me to Dan's wife, Dan's mother, Dan's father, Dan's sister, and a few other family members as well. I awkwardly handed over the helmet and the backpack to Dan's wife, Adrian.

Adrian took a worn sweatshirt out of the backpack and proceeded to bring it to her face, burying her face in the soft fabric. She inhaled the scent of her husband's clothes, reminded of him by his scent. My heart ached as I watched her begin to weep.

For the next hour and a half, I sat with Dan's family and mourned with them. Of course, I did not know or love Dan like they did, but I felt their pain. I saw how loving this family was and it made me hurt even more. The family asked me all sorts of questions, wanting to know everything. I told them everything I could as gently as I was able.

Looking back, what really made me wonder was how this family seemed to be so incredibly at peace. I saw no signs of anger, no signs of bitterness, and no signs of hatred toward the man who had taken Dan's life. I only saw sadness.

The more we talked, the more I began to realize that this was indeed a family of believers—believers in a heavenly Father and believers in Jesus Christ. They were at peace because they knew Dan was in heaven. They felt no anger because of their faith in God. That evening, I was able to see a glimpse of an inner peace that shone as a bright light in the darkness. I did not understand it, but through their peace, I too was comforted for a moment. As soon as I drove away, that moment was gone and the darkness of faithless hopelessness shrouded my heart once again.

The image of the scene, the picture of Dan's body lying in its crumpled state on the side of the road, would continue to plague my thoughts. As usual, I turned to alcohol to numb the pain and the darkness. I just wanted to escape it all and never see again what I had seen. *What is the point of this life? What difference does it make? Who cares? We will all end up dead with no hope anyway.* Thoughts of despair surfaced in my mind more and more, and I was actually beginning to believe these lies of Satan.

A few weeks later, I received an envelope from the medical examiner's office. *Autopsy photos.* I knew I shouldn't look. I did anyway. The raw, grim, stark reality began to set in as I looked at those photos. The ultimate reminder of our fragility and mortality in this fallen, broken world. Death seemed to surround me everywhere I turned.

The drunk driver who took Dan's life was charged with aggravated involuntary manslaughter and ended up serving a couple of years in prison. I'll call him John. On the day John was sentenced, I saw his family in court, including his wife and his two teenage sons. I could not imagine what that family was going through. They weren't the *real* victims here. *They didn't have to deal with the death of a loved one*, I thought.

But John's family was heartbroken. The two boys and the loving wife of this man, sick with alcohol addiction, watched as John was sentenced to be in prison, away from his family for the next two years. Those two boys would be without their father because of a decision he made.

This really scared me as I thought of my own alcohol problem. I had denied that I was an alcoholic for years. I would never kill anyone, I thought. I would never drive drunk. So that made me better than John, right? I was only medicating my pain—I wasn't hurting anyone else.

In reality, though, my family was suffering; they were victims of my alcoholism. Just like John's family, my family had no idea that I drank heavily every night. They didn't know that, at times, I would drink to the point that I would vomit. They didn't know why I was so incredibly short-tempered and angry with them all of the time; why I yelled at them and treated them so poorly. They didn't know—but they kept loving me anyway.

— 10 —

Help Me

This is the hardest part of this book for me to write—the beginning of the darkest time in my life. My marriage continued to survive, although barely. Stacy and I hardly ever saw each other. She was a high school teacher and often left the house at 6:30 a.m. Many mornings, it would still be dark outside, long before I got up. Hung over every day, I slept in as much as I could. I would take our daughter, Ana, to daycare at some point late in the morning after waking up late (as little Ana sat in bed with me and watched *Sesame Street*). After dropping Ana off, I would come back home and get ready for work, hitting the street for the beginning of my shift at twelve noon.

Coming home from work after 8:30 p.m., Ana would be asleep, and I would wait for my wife to go to bed so I could start drinking. I would be up until the early morning hours, drinking until I could barely walk straight. I had no purpose, no ambition, and I was trapped in misery as alcohol's clutches gripped me tighter every day. I was constantly in a foggy haze, blinded and dulled by the effects of drunkenness. My body ached and my mind was in a constant stupor.

We were pregnant with our second child. Early on in the pregnancy, there were warning signs of trouble. Stacy was bleeding a lot, and we were both worried. Even though, deep down, I could not imagine bringing another life into this world, I hoped that maybe I could change. The doctors told Stacy to take it easy and eventually placed her on ten days mandatory bed rest. My mind was in such a dulled state of clarity from my excessive drinking. I didn't think anything of it.

I remember one of our first doctor's appointments with this new pregnancy. It was absolutely a reflection of our relationship at the time. This was supposed to be a happy time, to see the first pictures of our second child with the ultrasound machine. Instead, we spent most of our time arguing as a result of my bad attitude and my heart of stone. We decided that we would wait until birth to see if the baby was a boy or a girl, just like we did when we were expecting Ana to be born. I don't remember going to any more doctor's appointments after that. After the way I had acted, I wasn't so sure I would be welcome.

Stacy was in her twentieth week of the problematic pregnancy. I have read that at fourteen weeks, the brain impulses in an unborn baby begin to fire. At fifteen weeks, the unborn baby can sense light. At nineteen weeks, the baby's senses are all developing—smell, vision, touch, taste, and hearing. It is on the nineteenth week that pregnancy books tell you to play music, sing, or read aloud to your baby. At twenty weeks, a fetus measures around ten inches from head to heel. I had already felt the baby kick several times, and I was actually starting to get used to the idea that another little one was going to be joining our family. Perhaps a new life would mean new hope.

All I can remember of that day is that Stacy was in so much pain. We had called the doctor who thought it to be constipation. My mother was over as well after a long day of Stacy being in pain. It was Sunday, October 20, 2013, around 8:00 p.m. I was so bitter, so angry, and filled with darkness. My mind was so clouded with numb indifference from the usual drinking. I cannot provide much recollection of the details prior to this moment. Stacy was again on bedrest, and I listened to her wailing in pain across the house. Suddenly, she started crying, "Somebody help me! Someone *please help!*" My wife pleaded in desperation to anyone who would listen, the agony in her voice was unbearable.

Instead of helping my wife, I stood there. *She'll be fine. What can I do anyway?* My mother immediately answered the calls for help as I remained still, motionless, and heartless. Careless and bitter, I glared at my mother-in-law who had just come into the house.

"She's fine," I announced in an icy tone. My mother-in-law, Dawn, pushed her way past me to check on her daughter as Stacy continued to cry out.

Moments later, as Dawn reappeared with a panic in her eyes, the words coming out of her mouth obliterated what little feeling I had left. "Stacy passed the baby!"

I dropped to my knees right there in the kitchen. "I can't do this anymore!" I said it out loud. My heart was already in such a dark place, and now Satan had whatever small piece of my soul I hadn't already given to him. I somehow managed to grab a telephone and call 911 before collapsing on the floor. It's all I could do. I couldn't even go in and check on my wife. I was so afraid of what I would see; my fear kept me away.

Ana was three years old. She was about to turn four in just nine days. I don't remember where she was before hell made its way into our home that day, but suddenly she was there, repeating what Dawn had just said. "Stacy passed the baby! Stacy passed the baby!" My sweet little baby girl had no idea what she was saying or the devastation behind it. I quickly scooped her up from where she was standing, just outside the bathroom where Stacy was screaming in pain. I could hear my mother instructing Dawn on how to assist with completing the delivery of the baby. I didn't want Ana to see what was in that bathroom and I had to rescue her from the horror. I didn't want to see it either.

Carrying my three-year-old little girl, already beginning to fight the tears as they streamed down my cheeks, I pushed my way outside and made my way to the house next door. Stacy's parents lived right next door to us, something I wasn't too crazy about in my dark state of heart and mind. In the brisk October air, I passed my daughter over to my father-in-law, Lowell, and tried to explain to him what was happening; but I could not speak. I was overwhelmed with sadness. I was losing a child, Ana was losing a little brother or sister, and Lowell was losing a grandchild. There was no need for words.

I could hear the wail of sirens long before I saw the first sign of an ambulance. *Maybe they can save the child…* but the thought only lasted a split-second. I didn't know much about pregnancy, but I knew that a baby couldn't survive outside the womb at twenty weeks. There was no hope.

I remember a deputy sheriff named Stephen showing up before the ambulance. Stephen was scanning the rescue squad's channel and heard my name over the radio. Stephen knew me and decided to respond. As the paramedics made their way up the steps into my home to tend to my wife, Stephen stood with me and embraced me as I cried. I felt the cardboard stiffness of his bullet proof vest as my arms collapsed around his uniform. Stephen was a tough guy who I never would have expected to comfort me in my moment of weakness. It felt good to have someone there who cared. He kept telling me, "You're tough. You're tough. You are one of the toughest guys I know…"

Well, I didn't want to be tough anymore. And I didn't feel very tough at that moment. It was dark outside as I stood there with Stephen. Inside, it was dark in my heart. *How could God do this to me?*

After what seemed to be an eternity, the rescue squad was wheeling Stacy out of the house on a stretcher. She was being transported to Martha Jefferson Hospital. My mother would later tell me how she tried to see if the baby would respond, but the baby was gone. As she told me this, my heart ached so badly. I just wanted to die. *Why not me instead?*

Physically, Stacy would be okay. She would have to spend that night in the hospital but was released the next day in the afternoon. I went home later that night, since Stacy was staying at the hospital, and I drank. Drinking would make it all better. Numbing the pain in my heart would fix everything. After getting drunk, I collapsed in my bed, hoping that I did not wake up.

Christian

"*Someone help me… please!*"

I awoke from the nightmare in a sweat as the alcohol oozed from my pores. I rolled over, looking at the empty half of the bed next to me where Stacy slept, and reality came back like a slap in the face. I allowed the darkness to take me back as I closed my eyes.

The following day, I remember returning to the hospital just before noon (I wasn't about to get up early and go visit my wife; I was too hung over). So many thoughts were running through my mind. *Is this real? This can't be real.*

The nurses tried to help Stacy and me in our time of mourning, but the little informational pamphlets they awkwardly handed us didn't help much. They gave us a small box with a newborn baby's hat and a receiving baby blanket. I wanted to push it away in disgust and anger, but I accepted the token of sympathy as graciously as I could.

The nurse asked if we wanted to know if the baby was a boy or a girl. We had the nurse write down the sex of our child on a little yellow piece of paper so that we could read it when we were ready. I hurriedly stuffed the neatly folded paper into the box with the tiny little hat and blanket and quickly closed the lid.

The people from the hospital wanted to know what we wanted to do with the body. *Really? We just lost our child. Will you just leave us alone so we can grieve in peace?* They also asked us if we wanted to see the child. I know they were only trying to help, but I didn't want to deal with any more death. A small part of me yearned to see the sweet precious baby that we had lost. But I wasn't strong enough.

I thought back to when I was twelve years old, wanting to see my father's body after he had passed away. My mother's words echoed in my mind, *"He's just a shell now, his soul has gone to heaven."* The death that surrounded me had now surrounded my family as well. I just wanted to crawl into the darkest place I could find and never come out.

When Stacy and I finally returned home that afternoon, the house was so quiet. I could barely look my wife in the eyes. I was so ashamed for the way I had acted when Stacy was going through such trauma. What a heartless coward I had been. I was stricken with guilt.

She would later tell me that she was on the toilet, in incredible amounts of pain, thinking she had bad gas. Suddenly, she looked down and saw a tiny foot sticking out. She said that after that, she didn't look anymore. When her mother came in, she would later tell me that she looked her mother in the eye and said, "Jon has lost his faith."

We asked a pastor from Stacy's childhood church to come to our home two days later. Pastor Norm Johnson had baptized Ana when she was a baby. I remember Norm sitting across the table from me as I sat in my world of despair. Norm was a soft spoken man in his fifties with short gray hair, gold wire-rimmed glasses, and kind blue eyes. Norm tried to comfort us the best that he could, but his words were empty to me.

We asked if Pastor Norm would read the little yellow slip of paper that would tell us if we lost a son or a daughter. Norm pulled the paper out of the little box and carefully unfolded it. "Are you ready?" he asked.

I nodded my head as I looked over at Stacy. My emotions were about to take over; of course, I wasn't ready. I would *never* be ready to hear what he was about to say. "The baby was a little boy," he said softly. I immediately began to sob. My mind was overwhelmed with grief and sadness. I felt like a spear had just pierced my soul. *My son. My first born son was dead.*

Stacy spoke in a calm and reassuring voice. "I knew it was a baby boy. I had a dream last night, and God told me his name is Christian."

Christian. Somehow, I knew it too. I simply gave a slight nod of my head in agreement. Pastor Norm prayed with us. I felt so far from God, but I closed my eyes and prayed too.

And so we began planning Christian's memorial service and working out the details of what to do with Christian's body. I immediately began to feel the heavy burden of carrying a new and deep sadness with me. At the age of thirty-four, I had buried my father, and now I was facing the reality of having to decide if I was going to bury my son. We decided to cremate Christian's body.

I remember being on the phone with the funeral home that we had chosen to cremate Christian. I was enraged at the fact that I had to pay (a large amount) for this. I felt like I shouldn't have to pay anything. A few days later, I would receive a call that the bill had been taken care of. I didn't know it at the time, but my mother had paid the bill for us. I was grateful to have one less thing to worry about.

The memorial service was held that Thursday night in Pastor Norm's small country church in North Garden. In so many ways, this little church was like the little country church that Stacy and I used to attend before we were married. That seemed like so long ago, and I was such a different person now. Several people from the police department came and, of course, family and friends. I sat in the front row and sobbed and sobbed with my head down for most of the service. My eyes were so blurred with tears, I couldn't see much anyway. I felt like I was reliving the memorial service from so many years ago when my dad died. Surely nothing good could ever come from this.

The service ended with a beautiful delivery of "Amazing Grace" by Mary Anna, a young woman who worked as a civilian employee at the police department. As Mary Anna's hands danced across the keys of the old church piano, I cried harder than I had cried in a long time. I was so overcome with sadness, darkness, and hopelessness. I know I wasn't the only one having a hard time with the loss, but I felt like I was the only one who couldn't control it.

Following the service, a receiving line of people formed to express their sympathies. I hugged and shook hands over and over. I didn't know what to say or how to act, but I really didn't care. I thanked people for coming and pretended that I was a decent person. Suddenly, amidst all the apologetics, a seasoned detective from the police department, Phil, was standing in front of me with his wife. He looked me square in the eye and said the most profound thing I had heard since this horror had begun: "God won't give you nothing you can't handle, brother." I was immediately taken aback. I didn't know what he meant. I nodded, blinked the tears from my eyes, and kept shaking hands. Those words would stay with me and still stay with me to this day.

In the days that followed, I took a few weeks off from work. I tried to deal with the pain by keeping busy with projects around the house during the day. At night, I would abuse alcohol and drink heavily, desperately trying to numb the pain away. For a short time, Stacy and I felt close to each other and we would even spend time just holding each other. The loss we experienced together was bringing us close, but the closeness would quickly fade as I drifted back into my world of misery, alcoholism, depression, and darkness.

One day, I got the call that Christian's ashes were ready for pickup. Going to a funeral home and picking up the ashes of your baby is something that no one should ever have to do. The funeral home was nice enough to place the remains in a small wooden box, smaller than any trinket box I had ever seen. I remember driving home with that little box on my front seat, taking Christian home again. There are no words to describe the pain, the emotion, the sadness I felt. I didn't think I could ever recover from this devastation. The sadness I felt only added to the anger I already harbored in my heart.

A few officers from the department were compassionate enough to raise some donations for my family, and they used the money to buy a very nice Japanese cherry tree to plant in my yard. About a month after Christian died, I was diligently digging a hole to plant the new tree. It was the end of November and it was a terribly cold, terribly windy, clear day. The ground was still soft from recent rain, so the digging wasn't terrible. I had chosen a spot in my front yard so that the tree's beautiful white blossoms would be easily visible in the spring. My father in law, Lowell, came out to help me dig. Several officers from the department were coming later that day to help plant the tree, and I wanted to make sure the hole was dug before they came. I couldn't explain it, but I felt like I needed to be the one to dig the hole for the tree, almost as if I were preparing a burial site.

Lowell and I dug in silence. There wasn't much to say. Lowell, a military veteran, wasn't exactly about to start talking about sadness and feelings, but I knew he was hurting too. We concentrated on the task at hand, digging the hole about three feet wide and about two-and-a-half feet deep. Quietly and diligently, we prepared the site for Christian's memorial.

Soon, the officers from my department arrived along with the cherry tree. I counted fifteen officers who came out to help. I was amazed at the show of support, for I certainly did not feel that I was worthy or deserving of their compassion.

Randy, one of the officers assigned to the motor unit, had arranged for a beautiful memorial plate to be made that could be displayed in front of the tree. It was humbling; all these officers I worked with coming out to help plant this tree for my family and me. They carefully placed the tree into the hole that I had dug and patted potting soil and mulch around the top of the little tree's roots.

Randy handed me the memorial plate, the final touch. I pulled the bronze plate out of the box and read the engraved inscription, "This tree was planted in memory of Christian Everett Hickory, October 20, 2013. 'Before I formed you in the womb, I knew you'" (Jeremiah 1:5). On one side of the Bible verse was a tiny pair of handprints. On the other side of the Bible verse was a tiny pair of footprints. This memorial plate was so powerful and so perfect. I wanted so badly to believe that Christian was in heaven and that God knew him.

After giving the plate a careful polish, I eased the mounting stake into the ground in front of the tree and stepped back, admiring the memorial tree. I said a few words to all the officers standing around. I thanked them for being there, I thanked them for the tree, and I told them how honored I was to be a part of the police family. With my speech over, I invited everyone inside for coffee to get out of the cold. And so began the darkest time in my life I have ever known.

12

Self-Destruct

I felt so lost. I knew I was in a dark place before the loss of Christian. But now, for the first time in my life, I really began to question whether God even existed. I ignored all the blessings that I had, like my wife, my daughter, my family, my job, my home, and my health. I began to try to fix the dark hole in my heart by patching it with all the things of this world.

If it was even possible, I began to drink more heavily than before. I tried going to the gym more to get my mind off my misery. I began listening to music I had never listened to before—dark, heavy rock music and music that played on the popular "Top 40" stations.

I remember working out furiously one night at the gym, so late that no one else was there. The buzzing fluorescent lights overhead did little to drown out the shadows clouding my mind. As I listened to the senseless noise being pumped into my earbuds, one of the "popular" songs came on, and the lyrics were filled with darkness. The song fueled the sick dark thoughts that were already rampant in my mind as the words encouraged me that I was unable to be saved from this hell. These kind of angry, disturbing lyrics were becoming my new normal. I actually felt like I could relate to what these lost artists were singing about. *This world is such a dark and broken place*, I thought.

I tried taking trips on my motorcycle to help me to feel better. I continued to busy myself around the house with meaningless little projects. I signed up for extra overtime at work. I tried to make sure that I never had a free moment to think about how much I hated my life and how much I hated myself.

My marriage was far from perfect before Stacy and I experienced the death of our second child, but now it was beginning to suffer even more heavily. I found that not being able to look my wife in the eye was becoming a constant for me. Perhaps it was the shame and guilt I felt for not being there for her on that horrific day. Was I blaming her for this? Or was I blaming God? Or maybe I was blaming myself. Maybe God was making sure that I knew how much of a failure I was to Him and to my family, and God wouldn't give me "something I couldn't handle." The words that Phil had spoken to me at Christian's Memorial Service echoed in my mind, and the devil twisted those words like a knife into my heart. I tried to shut out all of my thoughts, but the more I tried to ignore my pain, the more it cried from within; the more it would not be silenced.

Stacy and I began to talk less and less. I became withdrawn, only communicating with her when it was absolutely necessary. The silence in our home was cold and lonely, like the death that had brought it on. I started to avoid my wife more and more and I began to feel uncomfortable being in the same room as her. I didn't understand why I was feeling this way, I didn't understand why I felt so empty, and I felt like life was hardly worth living anymore.

As time wore on, I withdrew from all the good in my life. I withdrew from my family, my wife, my daughter, and my friends. Anger consumed me as I lashed out at everyone who happened to get in my way or tried to reach out to me. It was like my life was the Starship Enterprise and I had pushed the self-destruct button with no way to stop it.

I adamantly refused to go to church. I remember one day at work, I went into the mail room to check my mailbox. The mail room at the police department is a small room with office supplies, the copy machine, and hundreds of small mailboxes for all of the officers and civilian employees. I walked in and saw some bright colored candy in my mailbox. Curious, I picked up the candy. As surrounded by darkness as I was at the time, I still had time to satisfy my sweet tooth, apparently. Attached to the candy-bait was an invitation to a church called The Point. I'm pretty sure it was an Easter invite, which would explain the candy.

Suddenly I was filled with anger, and I balled my fists in rage. I guess someone thought I needed to go to church! Well, I didn't need church! It was the last thing I needed! What was church going to do for me? God had already taken my father and my son from me! Burning with fury, I tore up the invite and threw it into the trash. *That will show them.* I kept the candy because I may have been angry, but I wasn't completely crazy.

Not long after the candy-invitation destruction, my supervising sergeant started to talk to me about church. He asked me to check out some of the messages available online from some pastor named

Andy Stanley. My supervisor knew what had happened and asked if I was doing all right. Not wanting anyone to know that I was hurting, I became offended at his concern for me. I told him I was fine and I didn't need anything and I certainly didn't need church. The sergeant was really trying to get me to listen to him, because he knew I was in pain. I tried to act tough, and I'm sure my sergeant could see right through it. He was trying to help me, but I was too stubborn and prideful to allow him past the walls I had put up around my heart of stone.

I refused to see the positive side of anything. I refused to laugh (unless it was at a filthy joke) and I refused to smile. I remained in a fog comprised of Satan's lies, alcohol, and misery. I became more and more cynical and I became more and more angry. My everyday language became filled with curse words and filth.

In May of 2014, I was given the prestigious award of Officer of the Year by the police department. A top award in a department of over 140 officers, I should have been proud of my accomplishment and honored to receive the accolade. Instead, I didn't even tell my wife about it and only attended the awards ceremony because I felt like I had to. I didn't care about being recognized. There was absolutely nothing in the world that brought me happiness.

As I continued to sink into darkness, and as I felt myself withdrawing more and more from my marriage and my family, I began to justify other forms of self-glorification. I refuse to glorify this deepest darkest vile sin, but I turned to pornography and I was also unfaithful to my wife. It sickens me to write about this, to relive the horrors of my adulterous sin as I write this chapter. Unfortunately, this was part of my complete self-destruction as I began to refuse to acknowledge the existence of God.

"Hurting people hurt people," someone once said. I can attest to this, for I hurt so many people as I sought pleasure and prideful things to cure my pain. Every woman I saw became a target of my ever increasing despicable lust.

Eighteen months of absolute hell followed the loss of my son. Not just personal hell for me, but for my wife and daughter and anyone else I was close to. Hell for my mother, and hell for Stacy's parents. No one wanted to see me hurting. But no one could help me. I was headed for an early death, in the fast lane on the highway to hell. But I wasn't going to die of cancer like my father; cirrhosis of the liver would likely be what would kill me.

Through all these hard times, Stacy somehow kept it together. She was going to church without me as I absolutely refused to go. She also surrounded herself with women who were strong in their faith in God. These women encouraged her and lifted her up and joined her in prayer. Stacy tried, in vain, to get me to see the blessings in my life. I responded with hurtful things and sarcastic remarks. I was lying to her every day, and if she knew the truth about my infidelity, I knew she would leave me. I knew Stacy was not happy, but she never seemed to hurt from this like I did. Stacy never turned to substance abuse and never became angry. Stacy never withdrew from me, and Stacy never gave up on life like I had. Stacy's faith was being tested, but God was carrying her through, day by day.

I would come to bed, night after night, and pass out in a drunken coma in the bed next to my wife. I figured Stacy was asleep, but she wasn't. Though I had absolutely no idea that this was happening,

Stacy would later tell me that after I would come to bed and drift into my drunken sleep, she would pray over me. Sometimes, Stacy would get out of bed, get on her knees, and pray that her husband would come back… that I would just come back to her.

It had been eighteen months since Christian died. In the month of April of 2015, our broken little family took a vacation to Disney World. Our daughter, Ana, was now five years old and she knew all of the Disney princesses by heart (quite a feat). This was a wonderful time to take her to the amazing world of Walt Disney, and Stacy had pinched and saved her money to pay for an extravagant two-week vacation in Orlando. I remember that I didn't even want to go. If I had to go to Disney World, that meant I would have to figure a way to hide my drinking while in a hotel room with my family. To me, this was a deal breaker. I was given the choice between my wife and daughter who loved me and alcohol. I chose alcohol.

But in the end, I ended up going (reluctantly). I stocked up on liquor and tucked a few extra bottles into my suitcase. We packed up the car and began the long drive south. Driving from central Virginia to Orlando is about a twelve-hour trip, and so Stacy had come up with the idea to divide the trip into two legs—six hours one day and six hours the next.

With a five-year-old, as anyone who has tried a long road trip with small children knows, twelve hours in a car is long time. Little bladders mean that children have to stop for bathroom breaks a lot more frequently, and so a six-hour trip can quickly become seven or eight hours. Not to mention the other important stops like coffee, fuel, lunch, etc. We finally landed in a hotel in South Carolina for the night. As I began drinking in the hotel room, I remember my little girl asking me what I was drinking and why it smelled so bad. Ashamed, I just ignored her and continued to drink.

The next morning, I groggily dragged myself out of the hotel bed with the stench of last night's rum still rolling off my breath. Stacy and Ana were all packed; Ana's tiny pink suitcase lined up neatly at the door next to Stacy's luggage, all ready to go. Ana was *so* excited that she was on her way to this magical place. They were waiting for me, and I was certainly in no hurry to please anyone. After all, they were *lucky* I even came along, I thought to myself.

After an argument during breakfast over nothing important, I said something awful and unmentionable to my wife and we loaded into the car in silence. The clanking of my liquor bottles as I set my suitcase into the trunk was the only sound to be heard. I couldn't wait to get to Disney World so I could retreat into another hotel room and start drinking again.

We finally pulled into the Animal Kingdom Lodge between 8:00 and 9:00 p.m. It was beginning to get dark, and we were all exhausted. We found our way to the lobby and were soon making the half mile walk to our room. The Animal Kingdom Lodge is African Safari themed and stretched for thousands of square feet. Stacy had really gone all out. We had a room at a Disney Resort with real giraffes just outside the window. My amazing wife was really trying to bring Ana happiness through this visit to the land of magic and she had spared no expense.

After we all settled in for the night, and after Ana had finally fallen asleep despite her excitement to visit the wonderful world of Cinderella and all the other princesses, I began to drink again. I drank until I couldn't stay awake any longer and passed out.

We started early the next morning. Stacy had filled our itineraries daily to maximize all the things that Ana was able to see and do. We rode a bus into the Animal Kingdom, and Stacy told me all that she could smell was alcohol coming from my breath. Embarrassed, I became angry and tried not to breathe in her direction. Most of the day was filled with my complaints and bickering as we tried to navigate our way through the theme park. I was ruining my daughter's trip to Disney World, but she didn't notice. Ana was so happy to be surrounded by all the things of her innocent fantasies—princesses, castles, fairy-tales, and animals.

The next morning, we all sat down to breakfast together at one of the Animal Kingdom Resort's many restaurants. I was hung over again from drinking in the hotel room. The rum and vodka cocktail was still strong on my breath as I struggled to maintain interest while we discussed the agenda for the day. I stared blankly at the nearby pool, poking at the runny eggs on my plate.

I should have been enjoying a wonderful time with my family. I should have been enjoying the magic of this animated adventure park like when I was a kid. Instead, I was lost in my own misery and darkness. I felt worthless. I was so tired of feeling tired and I hated who I was. Suddenly, I said something disrespectful and condescending to Stacy, snapping at her as she tried to include me in our family's plans for the day.

"*I hate you.*" Stacy's stinging words got my attention.

"What?" Like I didn't hear her.

"*I hate you. Everything* you *ever* say is mean, and we *don't deserve* to be treated like this! We are your *family!*" Stacy had tears in her eyes. Of course she meant it. Instead of lashing back, I pondered her words for a moment, and it was almost as if someone had finally flipped a switch. I felt like I had been slapped in the face. But she was *right*. Something needed to change. I was a monster, I hated myself, and I was destroying my life and hers.

Awakening

The rest of the Disney World vacation went by quickly. I laid low after that moment at breakfast. My wife had never told me she hated me before. It hurt even more that she had said it in front of our sweet little girl. But it needed to be said. I had been hurting everyone around me for a long time, and *enough* was *enough*. Looking back, I am proud of Stacy for saying what she did. It finally got me to begin to wake up. Stacy would later tell me that I had finally pushed her to her breaking point at that moment.

We made it back home to Virginia, driving the whole trip in one day. I remember that we were on the road for over fourteen hours, and I even got pulled over for speeding. We had just crossed the Virginia state line and I was going a lot faster than I should have been in my black Volkswagen Passat turbo diesel. We have all been there—a long road trip, several hours on the road, and you reach the home stretch and just can't get there fast enough! I saw the police car sitting in the median as I rounded a curve on that lone stretch of interstate, and as I passed the ominous cruiser, I looked down at my speedometer and… too late. You would think I would be better at avoiding these types of situations, but I just wanted to get home at that point. It was humbling and humiliating to be pulled over by another police officer.

Hoping the officer would somehow forget about my vehicle, I slowed to below the speed limit and moved over to the right lane, like a defeated dog tucking its tail between his legs and slinking away. As the flashing blues came barreling down the dark roadway behind me like a lightning storm in the night, I knew they were for me. The vibrating pulse of the rumble strip reverberated throughout the car as I proceeded to pull over onto the shoulder. By now, the cruiser was on my tail, and the officer still had not turned off the siren. I was worried my sleeping daughter would wake up, but thankfully she was still dreaming of Ariel, Cinderella, Snow White, and the rest of the princess crew. Finally, the siren clicked off and the officer made his way up to my driver door.

I watched his approach. This wasn't a state trooper. This was a local deputy of some sort. I could tell he was all business and seemed annoyed already with his gruff grimace and determined stare. I wondered if people felt like that when I pulled them over. Unexpectedly, I felt like I had no control. I had my wallet out to retrieve my driver's license and now, suddenly, I was so discombobulated, I could not find my license. After looking for what seemed like thirty seconds, Stacy kindly pointed out that the license was literally right under my nose. I may have accidentally shown the deputy my badge as well, which just happened to be readily available and a lot easier to find than that elusive license. I was fortunate and blessed enough to be given a warning, but I know I deserved a ticket. I slowed down for the rest of the trip.

I returned to work the following day. While I was in court that Monday, my phone started ringing like crazy. It was my sergeant. He called me twice within twenty minutes and left a voicemail that I needed to report to the police department immediately. As I listened to that message, I suddenly felt sick. *Very* sick. I knew. I knew what was coming and I was suddenly stricken with fear.

Once I finished up with my court cases, I began the long drive to the police department. The PD is only about ten to fifteen minutes away from the courts, depending on traffic. This drive was different. I knew I was in trouble. I could sense it in the tone of my sergeant's voice in his message. I just had this feeling… my extramarital adulterous behavior had finally caught up with me. I was so sick—I didn't know what was going to happen to me. Was I going to lose my job? How would I provide for my family? Why had I done such foolish and hurtful and evil things? Truthfully, my biggest fear was that my wife was going to find out that I had been unfaithful. Anxiety, worry, and absolute panic took over my thoughts.

I arrived at the police department and I was met by a sergeant who promptly took me to meet with an internal affairs lieutenant. This was worse than having to go to the principal's office back in elementary school… but I had that same sick feeling in my pit of my stomach. I felt like I was going to throw up, and for once, it wasn't from drinking too much. A voice recorder was placed on the table in front of me and I was told that I was being investigated for conduct unbecoming of an officer. I had to turn in my department issued laptop and cell phone at once and provide lock codes and passwords for the electronic devices. I was told I could continue to work but that I was not to discuss the investigation with anyone in the agency.

I was able to go home early that day. I was thankful, because the last thing I felt like doing was working. The house was empty when I got there. I laid on the bed and my mind swirled with panic. The fear of losing my job, my marriage, and my daughter consumed me. Why had I done such *stupid* things? Why would I risk all the good things in my life for selfish, momentary, sinful things? What else did I have to live for if I lost everything I had? I felt such despair and I had no answers. I couldn't bear these burdens any longer and I had nowhere to turn.

During those desolate moments, lying on that bed, for the first time in my life, I thought about killing myself. *Just end it all, right now.* The thought entered my mind for a second and I suddenly felt so gripped by evil and complete darkness. I felt like I was looking straight into hell itself. I quickly dismissed the evil thought from my mind and vowed never to allow this evil into my thoughts again. I could feel the presence of a dark, demonic, sinister spirit in the room with me. Ephesians 6:12 says, "For we do not wrestle against flesh and blood, but against the rulers, against the authorities, against the cosmic powers over this present darkness, against the spiritual forces of evil in the heavenly places" (NIV).

Even though I had not acknowledged the presence of God for a long time, I knew that someone was battling for my soul at that very moment. *I can't do this anymore*, I thought. If God was trying to get my attention, He definitely had it. I had finally reached my point of absolute desperation, my breaking point. I was an alcoholic, an adulterer, plagued by lust, miserable, ashamed, fearful, depressed, despondent, filled with hopelessness, consumed with anger, stricken with grief, and a failure to my wife and daughter. My head hung low in shame.

As soon as Stacy came home, I told her I wanted to start going to church with her. I'll never forget the look on her face. You would have thought she had seen a ghost. She didn't know quite how to take it. Stunned, she agreed, and the following Sunday we all went as a family to the church that Stacy had been going to since Christian died. The name of the church? The Point—the same church that I had found a mysterious invitation to in my mailbox at the police department over a year ago. I should mention there are well over one hundred churches in the Charlottesville area. I had never made the connection before, but looking back, I can see how God was working in my life, even when I refused to see Him.

I remember being anxious about my first Sunday at church. I hoped so desperately that I could find the answers I was looking for. I just needed someone to pray for me. I put on some "churchy" clothes, consisting of blue jeans and a polo shirt, and made sure to leave with plenty of time to spare. The church didn't own a building at that time and was meeting in the auditorium of a local high school. Stacy, Ana, and I pulled into the parking lot on that Sunday in late May 2015. The red banners with The Point's logo on it had big bold letters, reading, "Love God, Love People, Love Life."

Another sign read, "First Time Visitors, Turn on Your Flashers for VIP Parking!" It was all a bit overwhelming, but I did feel like I was being welcome with open arms.

After parking the car, I remember being greeted by someone at the door. The greeter had a cheery smile on her face and seemed genuinely happy to hold the door for my family and me. I walked into the lobby area outside the auditorium and I was surrounded by a presence I had not felt in a long, long time. Everyone was bustling about, some were serving coffee, and others were handing out note-taking materials for the service. Everyone in the church seemed so alive as if they had a light inside of them that is uncommon to so many in the world. I could not explain it and I did not try to understand it; I was just happy to feel the message that the church was very loudly exclaiming—come as you are. We took Ana to the church's version of Sunday school, which the church called Kid's Point, and then Stacy and I made our way into the auditorium.

We made our way to a seat and sat down inside the auditorium, waiting for the service to begin. We must have been early… either that or everyone else was late, because the place seemed to have a lot of empty seats. I looked around and saw what great lengths the church had gone through to transform this run-of-the-mill high school auditorium into a worship-centered sanctuary. From black drapes hung with aluminum pipe frames to elaborate LED stage lighting—it was easy to forget you were actually in the same place where countless high school plays and theater productions take place.

As I took in this wondrous transformation around me, I saw him coming a mile away. The pastor was making a beeline for Stacy and me. I rolled my eyes. *Here we go*, I thought. The last thing I needed was to have the attention on me. Suddenly, I wanted to jump up and run as fast as I could out the door, into the parking lot, and burn rubber all the way into the sunset. Too late! I froze in my seat.

"Hey, I'm Gabe!" The pastor's twinkling eyes and genuine warm smile quickly broke down a small part of the wall guarding my stone heart as I reluctantly shook his hand. Pastor Gabe Turner was a younger man than I thought; he appeared to be in his mid-thirties. His relaxed dress of boot cut blue jeans, a pastel purple-colored button down shirt, and stylish, worn brown leather brogue boots hardly suggested that he was the senior pastor of a church—at least in the churches I had been to. He had a presence filled with real joy and compassion that beamed from within. Pastor Gabe seemed to know Stacy already, and as I was introduced to the preacher man, I actually started to let some of my guard down. This guy really seemed to care, and I was hurting so badly inside, I was okay with that.

Soon after meeting Pastor Gabe, the worship music began and it was so beautiful to me. This was no lone piano or church organ with a choir—this was like being at a rock concert! Music has always played an important role in my life, and as I listened to the rhythms flowing from the stage before me, I could feel a soothing deep in my soul.

Pastor Gabe was in the middle of a series of messages (sermons) on the book of Mark. As he began to speak, I remember it seemed like he was talking to me the entire time. For the first time in years, I felt like I was beginning to see a glimpse of hope. Gabe said something that spoke to me specifically: "God has the final word on your pain." He then read a Bible verse from the book of 1 Peter, "And He Himself bore our sins in His body on the cross, so that we might die to sin and live to righteousness; for by His wounds you are healed." Gabe explained that if we accept Jesus, sin is no longer our master; our new master is righteousness.

He went on to read, "For you were continually straying like sheep, but now you have returned to the Shepherd and Guardian of your souls" (1 Peter 2:25).

Here I was, in the middle of all my sin and pain, crushed under the burdens I carried. Was it really so simple? After all I had done, slipping so far from God and any belief in Him as our good and faithful Father, could I really be forgiven of all my sin and delivered into righteousness just by accepting a relationship with Him? I knew I had been straying for a long time. It was time to return to the shepherd and guardian of my soul.

Gabe continued as I listened intently. "What we *do* need to understand is that when we follow Jesus, when we trust Jesus, there's a new category for our life. In fact, it's the only category for our life, and that category is not convenience, it's not comfort, it's not safe. The one category is for the sake of Jesus and for the sake of the Gospel. We no longer live for *ourselves*, we live for *Him* who died for us and rose again—who has saved us from our sin. And that means that the new mission of our lives is for the sake of Jesus and the sake of the Gospel."

At the end of the service, Pastor Gabe closed the service in prayer. In his prayer, Gabe solemnly prayed, "I pray God for our family this morning, for each one that's here that's going through a time unlike they've ever experienced before. May we experience your grace, may we experience the Gospel and the healing power of the Gospel on a level and a way that we have never known. God, may You reach deep into our hearts with Your grace and with Your power and bring healing to those who are hurting that are full of pain. And God, may You heal, by Your stripes we are healed. God we look to You, we trust You as we follow You, God, for Your sake and for the sake of the Gospel."

At the end of the prayer, Gabe opened an invitation to those who wanted to receive Jesus Christ into their hearts. He continued to pray, "Today you've heard the Gospel, the good news, and God is calling you to turn from your sin and repent and turn toward Him."

I couldn't pray the words fast enough! I was so ready to receive grace from my heavenly Father. I made my decision that day—I would commit to following Jesus Christ for the rest of my life. I was so tired of turning to alcohol and a life of sin, shrouded by darkness. I was weary from the hell of life without God.

I joined Pastor Gabe in praying these simple, life-changing words, "Heavenly Father, thank you for your Son, Jesus. Thank you for sending Him to die on the cross for my sin. Come into my heart, cleanse me of my sin. Help me to live for You from this day forward. In Jesus's name, Amen."

Immediately, I felt a change within me. It felt good to stand for something good. Now make no make mistake, I knew that this was not a magical instant change of who I was. I knew that this was going to take real commitment. But something had definitely changed. I was determined to start doing whatever I had to do, whatever it took to follow Jesus.

A few people stood in front of the stage at the end of the service, facing out into the crowd, and waiting expectantly. They almost looked like the security people at a rock concert. Despite the appearance of security personnel protecting the stage, their purpose was the complete opposite of keeping people away: this was the church's prayer team. Now came the fun part for me—I had to fight the masses of people (almost all of the seats had filled up in the auditorium) in order to get down to the stage to get prayer. I told Stacy I was making my way down, and I began to push my way past all the people who were leaving. I was on a mission and I just wanted to be obedient to God.

I finally made my way down to the stage and picked out one of the prayer people. I headed toward the one that looked like he was a little more seasoned than the rest, a kind looking man in his fifties with dark brown hair combed neatly into place. The nametag said "Rich Newsome, Care Pastor."

As I introduced myself, I hesitated. "Hi, I'm… Jonathan." I had hesitated because, for the first time, I had introduced myself with my full name, Jonathan. For my entire life, I had always introduced myself as "Jon," and that is what everyone called me.

I remembered the story of Saul of Tarsus in the Bible. According to the book of Acts, Saul used to persecute, hunt down, and imprison Christians. One day, Saul was on the road to Damascus when the Lord appeared to him in a bright light that caused him to fall face down on the ground. The Lord asked Saul, "Saul, Saul, why are you persecuting me?"

Saul was commanded to go to Damascus where he would end up proclaiming that Jesus is the Son of God. He was filled with the

Holy Spirit and committed his life to following Jesus. After his conversion, Saul was no longer called Saul, but Paul. Paul went on to be the most dramatic conversion in the Bible, writing thirteen books of the New Testament. Amazing. If there was hope for Paul, perhaps there was hope for me. Like Paul, I was a new man who had been reborn in Christ, so I wanted a new name. I resolved in that moment that I would no longer be Jon but Jonathan.

As I began to pour my heart out to this complete stranger, the tears would not stop flowing down my cheeks. I was amazed by how comforting a presence Rich had. This made it easier to feel I could trust him. He had that same light and peace coming from within him that I had seen in the pastor. The same peace I had seen when visiting Daniel's family on the night after his tragic death, even as they grieved. The same peace that Stacy had within her, despite the loss she had experienced and her husband (me) spiraling downward into darkness. This was the peace and inner light of the Holy Spirit, and it was something I longed for.

Rich prayed for me, and I remember him using words from scripture in his prayer, saying that God had removed my sins from me "as far as the east is from the west." I did not know this was scripture at the time, but Rich was referring to Psalm 103. I felt Rich's hand on my shoulder as I hung my head and let the tears flow. In that moment, I felt a great weight lifting from me. All of my burdens were no longer mine to carry. All of my pain, my suffering, my sin, my brokenness was gone as the grace of God washed my heart as white as snow.

This was the beginning of my walk with the Lord—my journey. And soon I would find out that when you have been marching with Satan and he loses you from his ranks, he doesn't give up so easily.

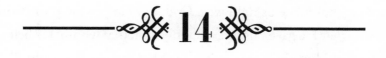

Signs

After Rich prayed for me in front of the stage, I made my way to a place in the lobby area outside the auditorium that the church cleverly called Connection Point. Connection Point was just a small table staffed by a couple of volunteers, but it had the monumental purpose of connecting people to the church. I picked up a copy of a little book with a gray cover called *Seek First, A New Believer Journal.* Inside the cover was the verse from which the title had been inspired. "But seek first His kingdom and His righteousness and all these things will be given to you as well" (Matthew 6:33, NIV).

As soon as I got home, I started reading. The book was a wonderful little journal and guide for me as I was so new to accepting Christ into my heart and making this life-changing decision and commitment to the Lord. A handbook for the wide-eyed new Christian, essentially. The book started off by outlining the facts:

- The Bible says we have all sinned and fall short of the glory of God. (Romans 3:23, NIV)

- The wages of sin is death, but the gift of God is eternal life through Christ Jesus our Lord. (Romans 6:23, NIV)

- Jesus made us right with God: For God so loved the world, that He gave His one and only Son, that whosoever believes in Him shall not perish but have eternal life. (John 3:16, NIV)

- That if you confess with your mouth, "Jesus is LORD," and believe in your heart that God raised Him from the dead, you will be saved. For it is with your heart that you believe and are justified, and it is with your mouth that you confess and are saved. (Romans 10:9–10, NIV)

The next passage of the book brought a new light to the meaning of baptism. Baptism? I was already baptized as a baby... why was it so important to be baptized? I began to read what the book said about baptism:

"Baptism is an opportunity for you to show everyone that you are now following Jesus Christ. Baptism doesn't make you a Christ-follower, but it is an acknowledgement that Jesus has changed your life. When you are baptized, you are dunked under water as a symbol of what Christ has done. It illustrates the death, burial, and resurrection of Jesus. It shows that you have trusted Jesus and that He has given you a brand new life. Baptism is your first act of obedience to Jesus. You'll want to get baptized as soon as possible."[1]

As soon as possible? Okay. I emailed the church and started asking about when I could get baptized. I was eager to take this obedient

---

[1] Marshall, Beth. *Seek First: A New Believer Journal.* Copyright 2002. Revised 2010.

step, no dawdling! I soon received a reply from an elder in the church named Dean Kurtz. Dean wanted to meet me for lunch or coffee before the church would baptize me. I guess he wanted to make sure this was for real. Maybe it was church policy or something. I met Dean a few days later over lunch at the local Chick-fil-A restaurant. Chick-fil-A seemed to be an appropriate location with the Christian-owned fast-food chain often being said to serve "the Lord's food."

Dean greeted me in the parking lot as he stepped out of his shiny red full-sized Ford pickup. Dean was a kind man with a gentle face. His gold-rimmed glasses gave him the appearance of a wise and seasoned man with a receding hairline and wispy brown hair. After ordering our chicken sandwiches with waffle fries, we sat down together at a small, somewhat private table. After Dean prayed over our meal, we began to talk about my acceptance of Jesus Christ. It wasn't easy to tell someone I barely knew about the darkness I had just stepped out of, but I knew that Dean only wanted to make sure I understood what it meant to profess Jesus Christ as my savior.

I began to tell Dean about my life. I shared how absolutely miserable I had been, how I self-destructed until I had nothing left and now, through Christ, I only wanted to be obedient and surrender to God. Dean listened quietly and intently, never interrupting. After I finished pouring out the wretched misery of who I had become, he pulled a small book with an army combat camouflage patterned cover from his shirt pocket. He placed the little book into my hands. It was a New Testament Bible, complete with the Psalms and Proverbs.

As I admired the gift, Dean spoke. "Jonathan, there is *absolutely* hope and a new life for you in a relationship with Jesus Christ.

Walking with Him, you will never be weary. Professing your faith by being baptized is a symbol of your commitment to the Lord."

I had been a bit vague in sharing on some of the details of my path of disintegration—behavior that haunted me. I wasn't so sure that anyone would want to baptize me, knowing the sins I had committed. The adultery, alcoholism, anger, darkness, selfishness. The deception of Satan was telling me to believe that no one needed to know what I had done, for if they knew, I would surely be outcast.

Dean and I wrapped up our lunchtime meeting with the plan that I would be baptized on June 7, 2015. There was another baptism Sunday available on May 31, but I had to work an overtime assignment for the police department that I had previously committed to. Being baptized on June 7 meant I would be traveling to the church's second campus about an hour away from my home. I was so ready to be baptized, to obey God—I didn't care if I had to drive all day to be baptized!

As I waited for this next step of baptism, it was everything I could do to make it through everyday life. With the open investigation into my conduct, I was fearful that I would lose my job. With the fear of losing my job came the fear of having to tell my wife of my infidelity, which made me fear that I was going to lose my wife and my daughter. I was so afraid, filled with the kind of fear that eats at you from the inside out. I was already beginning to lose weight from the anguish. Just getting out of bed every day and going to work was a labor filled with dread and anxiety.

In desperation, I pleaded with God to help me. *Please, Lord, save my job. Save my marriage. Help me to be a good father to my daughter. Please, God, help me. Lord, I promise to honor you with my life… please.*

In the Bible, Jonah prays a similar prayer in his hour of desperation. Jonah had been called by God to go to the great (evil) city of Nineveh and announce the Lord's judgement upon it. Instead of being obedient to the Lord, Jonah turned away from God and ran the best way he knew how by jumping the first ship out of town. Surprise, God wasn't too happy about Jonah's disobedience, and so He brought a great storm upon the sea that threatened to break the ship apart. Jonah knew that it was his fault the storm had come upon the ship, and so he talked to the other men on the ship: "Throw me into the sea," Jonah said, "and it will become calm again. I know that this terrible storm is all my fault" (Jonah 1:12, NLT).

The men finally agreed and threw Jonah overboard and the sea became calm. But Jonah wasn't out of the woods yet. "And the Lord appointed a great fish to swallow Jonah. And Jonah was in the belly of the fish three days and three nights" (Jonah 1:17, ESV).

I can imagine Jonah had a lot of time to think about what he had done and repent for his disobedience to the Lord. What did Jonah do from the stinking vile belly of the giant fish? He prayed to God. Jonah prays, "In my distress, I called to the LORD, AND HE ANSWERED ME. From deep in the realm of the dead I called for help, and you listened to my cry. You hurled me into the depths, into the very heart of the seas, and the currents swirled about me; all your waves and breakers swept over me. I said, 'I have been banished from your sight; yet I will look again toward your holy temple'" (Jonah 2:1–4, NIV).

After Jonah repents and prays to God, "the Lord spoke to the fish, and it vomited Jonah out upon the dry land" (Jonah 2:10, ESV). God hears Jonah's prayer and shows him mercy, despite his disobedient past. Jonah goes on to Nineveh as instructed, and the entire city repents of their evil ways!

I felt like Jonah in the belly of the great fish. God was displeased with my disobedience and life of sin. Sometimes, God will allow a crisis or something traumatic to get our attention when we are running from Him. He had sent a storm and a giant fish to get my attention, and I was calling out to Him in repentance.

Seeking reassurance in my new salvation, I was eager to tell a few officers at work who I knew were Christians. A few officers delighted in the news, and one even prayed for me on the spot. I felt so relieved that they believed in me, that perhaps there was hope for me. One day, in the middle of the waiting to see what my fate would be, I told another officer who gave me a very different response.

I was working that day in the Virginia heat of the afternoon in late May. I had just been involved in the apprehension of a suspect who was on the run. After a brief foot pursuit, I was drenched in sweat from the top of my head to the inside of my ballistic vest (tightly woven Kevlar wrapped in a plastic carrier doesn't breathe too well). Once the suspect was taken away from the scene by another officer (I was still assigned as a traffic officer and I did not have a transport cage), I spoke with the supervisor on scene. I'll call him Sergeant James.

James has always had the unique quality of speaking his mind, whether you like what he has to say or not. From previous conversations I had with him, I knew that James was a Christian. Excitedly, I shared the news of my acceptance of Jesus. James stared at me and didn't miss a beat or blink an eye, responding with the words, "That's great news, but keep in mind, it's going to get worse before it gets better."

I was dumbfounded, and I didn't really know how to take what he was saying. I respected him, but I felt like he was just brushing aside the amazement of my new salvation!

James seemed to sense my hesitation to agree with him, and so he explained. "You're going to be tested. Satan wants you back and he will fight... spiritual warfare."

Spiritual warfare? Maybe that's why I still felt like a piece of garbage, even though I had accepted Jesus into my heart. Satan was still fighting for me to believe his lies.

In the book *The Greatest Stories Ever Told,* Pastor Greg Laurie writes, "The devil is not happy with your decision to follow Christ. In fact, it enrages him! He's lost one of his own! But he's not going to take it lying down. He will hit back—hard. Someone has said, 'Conversion has made our hearts a battlefield.' The genuine believer may be known by his inward warfare as well as his inward peace. In fact, if you are not experiencing this spiritual tug-of-war, that in itself is cause for concern."[2]

As I continued to struggle through every minute, every hour, every day, I lived in fear. I continued to pray to God to help me, to

---

[2] Laurie, Greg. *The Greatest Stories Ever Told.* Kerygma Publishers, 2015. Page 103.

give me strength to carry on. I was still drinking, although I had tried to cut back some. I had good intentions, but I was weak, like a baby bird that had just left the nest for the first time. I was a newborn Christian. I had asked Christ into my heart, I loved Him, but I had no idea yet how to lean on Him, how to rest in His wisdom—to trust Him.

God would soon give me hope through three signs within thirty hours; signs that told me that He would take care of me. I just had to trust Him. May 29, 2015 would be our eleventh wedding anniversary, and I was reflecting on the kind of husband I had been to my wife. Satan was up to his usual deceit, filling my thoughts with self-condemnation.

My new eyes were wide open, just starting to learn to really see the world with a biblical view. Suddenly, I began to look up at the beautiful canvas of blue sky, the warm glow of the sunrise, the scarlet paintings of sunset, and all the beautiful plethora of landscapes around me as God's creation. I began to take notice of and appreciate the beauty of the world I lived in, the world that God had created.

On May 28, 2015, just after noon, I was pulling into the parking lot of one of my favorite restaurants to get some lunch. It had been less than two weeks since I had accepted Jesus Christ into my heart, and the fear of my fate was as fresh as my faith. A license plate on the back of an old beat-up Nissan Maxima caught my eye. As a police officer, I am always noticing license plates, and I usually dismiss them fairly quickly if there is nothing to warrant a second look. If I do give the plate a second look, it's usually because the plates are expired or they match the plate number of a recently stolen vehicle.

In Virginia, personalized license plates are everywhere, since they only cost an extra ten dollars on top of a normal registration fee every year. But this one spoke to me. This one stood out like an Olympic-sized swimming pool in the desert. The license plate read, "EPH 318." I knew enough about the Bible to know that this was referencing Ephesians 3:18, but I had no idea what Ephesians 3:18 said.

I had carefully placed the camouflaged New Testament that Dean had given me into the side pocket of my black canvas patrol gear bag that always sat in the front seat next to me. I snapped a quick picture of the license plate so I could reference it once I parked the cruiser safely. I eagerly started leafing through the little Bible until I found the book of Ephesians. As I made my way through the extremely thin and delicate pages, I finally found the verse. I read the verse over and over, and my eyes began to well with tears. "And may you have the power to understand, as all God's people should, how *wide*, how *long*, how *high*, and how *deep* his love is" (Ephesians 3:18, NLT).

I reveled in the words. Even though I felt like I did not deserve God's love, He still loved me. God loves all of His children. As I think back on the moment, I am reminded of the parable of the prodigal son in the gospel of Luke. Jesus tells a story about a wayward son who takes all of his inheritance from his father and goes off to a faraway land. The son spends all of his money on partying, prostitutes, and foolish living, and ends up so broke and desperate that he is forced to work feeding pigs. The son takes a hard look at his life and what he has become, and he realizes that even his father's servants have more bread and sustenance than he. He resolves to return to his father and repent, prepared to offer himself to be treated as a hired servant.

When the prodigal son returns home, he runs to his father and says, "I have sinned against heaven and before you. I am no longer worthy to be called your son."

Instead of rebuking his son, the father throws his arms around him and kisses him, calling for a fattened calf to be killed for a feast of celebration. In his joy, the father says, "My son was dead, but is alive again; he was lost, and is found."

God is *our* heavenly Father, and *I* was the prodigal son. I was so afraid of what would happen to me and so sure that God was going to cast me out or drive me away. But God was rejoicing and He had big plans for me! I just needed to have a little faith in His plan.

After getting off of work that day in late May, I was walking through the green grass between my wife's parents' house and my house. I happened to cast my gaze downward for a moment and I became transfixed on what I saw staring back at me from the ground. I crouched down in the grass and brushed my thumb over the unique creation lying so simply amongst the green turf. Yes, it was real: the largest four-leaf clover I had *ever* seen! I plucked it from where it lay nestled and admired the renowned sign of good luck. I heard God speaking to me very clearly through this sign, telling me that he would show me favor if I remained faithful and obedient. This was the first four-leaf clover I had ever found in my entire life on this green earth, and I was extremely excited in the discovery of such a thing and what it meant to me. God was using a worldly symbol of good fortune to speak His heavenly intentions.

The next day, May 29, 2015, was our wedding anniversary. I don't remember much about the day. After work, I went inside to change out of my uniform. I came back outside, shortly after 5:00 p.m. Pushing open the side door, I froze in my tracks. There in the driveway, right outside the door, looking up at me, was a beautiful, majestic painted turtle. I had lived at this house for nine years and I had never seen a turtle on the property, much less a turtle parked in the driveway right outside the house! Furthermore, I have never seen a turtle on the property since that day. After seeing two other clear signs from God within the past day, I knew this had to be another sign. I felt God telling me to be patient, because things would take time to get better.

Seeing all of these signs within thirty hours helped me to feel a little better. At the fledgling stage that my faith was developing in, I feel that God knew I needed something solid. A beacon of hope. Something that would speak to me in my infancy stage of faith and let me know that God would walk me through this, that He loves me, that He has great plans for me, and that in time, He would restore me completely.

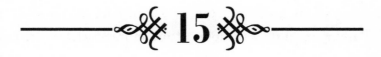

15

Obedience

For just a second or two, I couldn't breathe. The cold water rushed into my ears and tried to make its way into my nose as well. When I was lifted out of the cleansing water, the crowd that surrounded the baptismal erupted into applause and cheering. It was such an amazing feeling to be baptized, and I was relieved and filled with joy to know I was taking a step of obedience before God.

It was Sunday, June 7, 2015. Stacy was so excited to hear that I was going to be baptized. She had invited several of our closest friends and family. Over twenty of my Christian friends and family ended up showing for the church service and the baptism, along with a couple hundred more people that were in attendance of the preceding worship service. Don and Sheila Richardson, the loving disciples who had taken me under their wing early in life, even showed up along with their son, Scott, and his wife, Ginger. It was amazing to have the support of so many.

I remember changing my clothes after the church service that morning to get ready for my baptism. I was given a blue t-shirt from the church that said "I have decided" in large white capital letters. I also traded my blue jeans for a pair of swimming trunks. Dark thunderheads loomed overhead, and for a moment it appeared as if we were all about to get drenched. Thankfully, the only person who got wet that day was me.

I stepped into the small round pool that had just been filled by means of a nearby garden hose. The pool itself stood about three and a half feet high and was decorated with the tackiest azure blue pool pattern known to man. Ugly duckling though it may have been, it did the job, and that's all that mattered. The waist-deep water was cold, but I didn't care. Dean Kurtz stepped in beside me, along with Pastor Adam Schwenk of The Point's northern church campus. Pastor Adam had given the sermon just a few moments ago. The three of us stood there in the water together, looking out at the crowd before us.

"Jonathan, have you accepted Jesus Christ as your savior and believe that he died for your sins?" asked Pastor Adam.

"Yes!" I said as loudly as I could without yelling. I wanted everyone to hear and I wanted everyone to know.

"Is it your desire today to publicly declare that belief by being baptized?" Pastor Adam asked me.

"Yes." I tried to tone it down a bit, barely able to hold back my enthusiasm.

"Then it is my honor to baptize you in the name of the Father, the Son, and the Holy Spirit," Adam replied.

That was my cue to hold my nose, because it was dunk time! Dean and Adam submerged me by taking me backwards into the water. As they brought me up out of the cleansing basin, I felt like I was coming out into the world as a new creation. Like an ocean of forgiveness washing over me, my baptism truly declared that my heart belonged to Jesus. It felt amazing and wonderful to be able to profess my faith in front of everyone who was close to me, but especially to make public my commitment to God. This day would forever be etched as one of my most meaningful and significant memories.

The investigation into my adulterous sin took two full months before I would learn my fate. During this time, my mind was constantly whirring in anguish with the possibilities of what the future held. It helped to pray and talk to God. I looked forward to going to church every Sunday, and I was thirsty for more to feed my soul! I began listening to online sermons from Pastor Andy Stanley of North Point Community Church, and I also started seeking Christian music. I knew that the dark music I had been listening to in the past was only fueling my depression and I longed for a way to feel closer to God through song.

Before accepting Christ, I had always absolutely *loathed* Christian music. My mother would always try to listen to the local Christian radio station while we were riding in the car together, and not only would I immediately reach for the knob to tune into something else, but I would make it a point to announce my disgust for the music. I never really connected with the old hymns that I used to stumble through when going to traditional churches. Of course, I loved the ones everyone knows, like "Amazing Grace" and "How Great Thou Art," but there were so many that just didn't seem to flow for me. Part of the problem was probably my own inability to carry a tune, but the real problem was that my heart wasn't in the right place to hear the hymns for their spiritual value and message.

I started my Christian music journey with a Google search for "Christian rock with female lead vocalists." I also searched for "Christian rock bands." To my delight and surprise, the first search result I saw for Christian rock bands was a band called Skillet. Amazingly, I had already begun to listen to Skillet, as I had recently competed in a police motorcycle rodeo while the DJ played the Skillet song "Hero."

As a motor officer, I had the opportunity and privilege to participate in several police motorcycle rodeos. A police motorcycle rodeo is a way for motor officers from multiple police agencies to train together while involving some friendly competition. The public is invited to come out and watch, and in the case of the Albemarle County Police, the rodeo raised money to benefit a charity such as the local chapter of the SPCA or the Special Olympics. The Jefferson Area Motor Squad—made up of motor officers from the Albemarle County Police, Charlottesville City Police, and University of Virginia Police—has been hosting an annual police motorcycle rodeo since 2013.

In one of the competition events of the motorcycle rodeo, our motor officers ride a timed challenge cone course with as much speed and precision as possible. To make it fun, each officer gets to choose what song he/she wants to play while they ride (within reason, due to the presence of the public—no explicit lyrics). It's an exhilarating experience to have the crowd cheer you on as you hear the DJ blasting your favorite song on the loudspeakers for everyone to hear. The motor officer dips and dives with the motorcycle, negotiating through tight twisty turns of blazing orange cones, letting the snorting machine of steel and combustion rock back and forth beneath their torso. Officers would often choose classic songs like "Low Rider" and "Don't Stop Believing." Some officers would choose songs that reflected their personality, such as a country song. The song "Hero" by the band Skillet was my choice for the 2015 competition, which took place June 12–13, 2015.

I chose "Hero" because it inspired me. The amazing thing is that I chose the song before I knew that Skillet was a Christian rock band. Imagine mustering up the mental strength to compete in something that requires complete focus, skill, and balance, while the haunting thought that you might be about to lose your job dwells in your mind. The first few verses of the song spoke to me in my struggle, fiery lyrics depicting the darkness of this world and the devastating effect it has on our faith and our families. Then, the chorus refers to a hero—a savior who will swoop in and save the day. Give the song a listen if you've never heard it and you will enjoy a solid rock song!

What I did not realize, at the time I chose the song, was the hero they speak of in the song is Jesus Christ. We all need Jesus to save us—I desperately needed Jesus to save my life, and how powerful it was to me. Listening to the song after accepting Jesus into my heart, He *was* saving me, just in time. Jesus was indeed my hero.

The other Google search for Christian rock bands with female lead vocals stemmed from my appreciation of bands like Evanescence, a solid melancholic rock band with a female lead vocalist. This led me to discover Christian bands like Fireflight and The Letter Black. I could not believe how good these bands were! They completely *rocked!* I also began listening to a Christian female artist, Kari Jobe.

Her beautiful voice and hearing her sing "Forever" and "I Am Not Alone" brought hope to my heart and tears to my eyes. This began my transition to Christian music, and I never looked back (nor did I wish to look back) to the music I used to allow to influence my spirit.

When I was given the *Seek First* book at the Connection Point kiosk, the church also recommended that I attend a community group. More specifically, a men's Bible study group. One way that the church connected its people was through these groups. Different age groups, men's and women's groups, different geographical locations in the area, and even groups for married couples and singles made up the diverse variety of community groups. I was given information on the time and location of the men's group and began to attend soon after I accepted Christ into my heart.

I will never forget the first time I attended a men's group. I really had no idea what to expect, and I was a bit nervous, thinking that as a newcomer, I would be singled out and made to talk about myself. It was a Tuesday evening in late May 2015, a beautiful sunny day. I found the location with no problem. It was a community clubhouse of a residential neighborhood just outside the city of Charlottesville and actually very close to the local jail—needless to say, as a police officer, I was familiar with the area. The clubhouse was tucked away from the hustle and bustle of the main road, a quaint meeting place complete with a pool for the neighborhood residents.

I arrived a bit early, and after a deep breath, I walked in to the pastel yellow clubhouse. I stepped through the French doors into a small room with a couple of tired blue couches and a few chairs surrounding a worn wooden coffee table. There in the meeting room, preparing his notes, was the men's group leader, none other than Rich Newsome. I could hardly believe it! Looking back, I can see God at work. God led me to choose Rich the day that I went down to the stage in front of the church. At least Rich knew a little bit about my past. *Maybe he won't pry too much*, I thought. Rich welcomed me with enthusiasm, and I took my seat as other men began to arrive.

The seating pattern in the room reminded me of sitting around a dinner table. Rich was seated in the chair that would have been the "head" of the table. I guessed he sat in this seat so he could equally engage all of the men seated around the room. I sat immediately to Rich's right, seated in the corner of one of the shabby (but not shabby-chic) couches. As other "regulars" trickled in, they introduced themselves to me with a quick handshake. When these regulars greeted each other, they were doing crazy things like hugging each other! I saw the affection they showed to each other and immediately was leery of what kind of group this was.

At the time, I thought that men who hugged each other must be, well, hippies! Or some kind of soft non-manly stereotype. My heart had been hardened for so long, all I could think was the worst about people, and as a new Christian, the softening of my heart would take some time. At the same time, though, I felt a little left out. The more I saw the men interact with each other with such familiarity and brotherly love, I began to see that they genuinely cared for each other, and I wished that I was a part of the bond they shared.

My eyes then focused on a bigger barefooted guy who was seated across from me on the other couch. His name was John—big

John. Despite his macho build, John was one of the guys who had been doing lots of hugging, so I had already been watching him. He was like a grizzly bear hugging small trees. As John took his seat, I noticed a large sharp kitchen knife next to his sandals (I guess he didn't walk in barefoot) beneath the couch where he was sitting. One of those huge culinary knives with an eight-inch blade. The perfect weapon to start hacking away at all these unsuspecting Christians. The police officer inside of me started planning all sorts of scenarios that would take place with this gigantic butcher knife. What I had failed to notice was the enormous ripe watermelon that sat on a table in the back corner of the room. John had brought the watermelon to share with everyone and had brought the knife to slice it fresh. I felt like such an idiot when I finally made the connection.

Despite my initial uneasiness with the group, I continued to go back every week. I even began to look forward to going! I loved to hear the other men pray openly to God. Rich always began the formal part of the meetings with praises and prayers. One thing I noticed right away was that when he would ask if there were any praises, anything the men wanted to thank God for, it was always silent for a moment. Crickets could often be heard. Eventually, someone would think of something they were thankful for, such as a safe trip back from visiting family or a good visit to the doctor. But when Rich asked if there were any prayer requests, the men were always champing at the bit to announce their concerns—as was I. Oftentimes, the prayer requests would outnumber the praises ten to one. Week after week, this was something I observed. Praises were hard to come by and prayers were plentiful. I wondered, is this a reflection of the heart of man? Or is this a reflection of the world we live in? We are so consumed by the hardships and trials we face that the things we are thankful for often dip beneath the surface of our thoughts.

I asked the men to pray for me every week, because I was afraid what would happen with my job and my marriage. I didn't want them to know too much for fear they would judge me. I found comfort in hearing these godly men praying for me. I remember fidgeting from withdrawal symptoms and feeling guilty and shameful (that I was still drinking) as I sat in the group, still battling my addiction to alcohol. I was paranoid that these righteous brothers would see my fidgeting and know that I had not been able to defeat the enemy's strongest hold on me; that I had not yet learned to trust and allow God to take this addiction from me.

There was certainly something rewarding about spending time with these brothers in Christ. The more time I spent with this group of fellow believers, the more spiritually refreshing it was, and the more welcome I felt. What a stark contrast to the other men I normally spent time with. I was used to men who were largely cynical on life and weak in their faith; men who felt more comfortable tearing others down than building each other up. These men of faith were so different. They were unified in fellowship by their common belief in Jesus Christ and the love they shared for God and for each other.

I continued to pray, to talk to God, to plead with God. My faith settled my restlessness as I waited for that long two months. Some people gain weight under extreme stress, some people lose it. I lost fifteen pounds and I lost a lot of sleep. Unable or unwilling to flee from my flesh's addiction to alcohol, I continued to numb some of the anxiousness as well. One Friday morning in late June, 2015, I finally got notice that I was to meet with my lieutenant at two o'clock that afternoon.

Instantly, I was stricken with panic. I felt sick. I felt sure I was going to vomit. *This was it. God help me.* I did the only thing I knew I could do. I prayed. Hard. And then I went to the only place on earth I knew I could go for help—The Point Church office.

Just after lunch, in full uniform, I walked into the lobby area and spoke with a nice young lady behind the desk. The exchange went something like this:

"Can I help you, Officer?"

"Yes. I need a pastor."

"Is there something I can help with? Is there something going on?"

Oh yeah. I'm dressed as a cop. "Uh, no, I really need a pastor. I need someone to pray for me. Is there anyone here?"

"Pastor Dave is here, he's our worship pastor…"

"Great! That will be fine, thank you. I just need someone to pray for me, please."

The young lady disappeared into the back of the office space and returned with a hip-looking guy in his early thirties, complete with a well-trimmed, yet slightly grungy dark brown beard. *Where do I know this guy from?* I wondered. Then it clicked… worship pastor! Pastor Dave Herring was the guy who sang and played the guitar on stage at the church. I sure hoped he was qualified to pray and wasn't just a hip-looking musician that they gave a pastor title to. Little did I know what an amazing man Dave Herring was and what an incredible pastor he would turn out to be. God led me to Pastor Dave; Dave has a brother who is a police officer. Because he has a police officer in his immediate family, Dave was able to look beyond the uniform and speak to me.

Pastor Dave must have sensed the fear and uncertainty within me. He led me into a small private meeting room where we could talk. Little did I know it, but Pastor Dave thought that I was there on some sort of official business and was truly worried about what I was about to tell him. *Sorry about that, Pastor Dave.* Silly cop uniform.

I went on to tell Pastor Dave everything. I didn't spare the details this time. This was a man of God. A clergyman. A man of the cloth. I feared no judgement from Dave. His presence, his calm, his demeanor led me to just let it all out. Dave was truly meant to be a pastor, and just speaking with him helped me to feel better instantly. I told him of my past. I told him of my sin. I told him I was getting ready to discover my fate and be disciplined for my conduct. I told him that I was in fear of losing my job and I was in fear of losing my marriage.

Dave asked me if I was going to tell my wife what I had done, advocating my honesty. I couldn't answer. "I'm afraid to tell her," I spoke softly. "I'm afraid she will leave me."

We bowed our heads as Pastor Dave spoke to the only One who could help me. "Father, I thank you for Jonathan. I thank you for his salvation and for his faithfulness. Lord, we know that because of your forgiveness, his sin is as far from Jonathan now as the east is from the west. He's about to go to find out his worldly fate, Lord, and I pray that he would be able to keep his job. Let him not lose heart and remind him of your presence, God, even as he sits in this meeting. We love you and we praise you, Almighty Father, in Jesus's name, Amen."

Oh man, I felt so relieved! That one prayer lifted so much weight off of me. Pastor Dave had truly uplifted me. We continued to talk for a little while, and then I had to go. Dave asked me what time I had my meeting of fate so that he could pray at that time again. I thanked Dave and out the door I went. The spring in my step (albeit brief) felt wonderful, and I sang along with Kari Jobe's song "Forever" the entire way to the police department.

16

Consequence

I clutched the camouflaged little New Testament Bible that Dean Kurtz had given me as I walked into the lieutenant's office. I had prayed the entire way from the car to this office door. My heart was pounding. The gruff, seasoned lieutenant told me to shut the door and to have a seat. He took his seat directly across from me at a small table. I could tell by his mannerisms and his militant tone that he wasn't happy. My mind raced with uncertainty, but my soul was still. I knew that the Lord was with me. Pastor Dave was praying for me this very moment, and whatever happened to me in this moment, I knew God had a plan for me.

I sat quietly and listened to what my fate would be as the discipline was doled out. My highly coveted position as a motorcycle officer and traffic officer was no longer. The unmarked car was no longer. I was to be immediately reassigned to the Uniformed Patrol Division, midnight shift. My first shift would begin in less than thirty-six hours. There were a few other career achievements I had worked hard to earn that were also stripped from me, but the biggest blow to me was the reassignment. I hadn't lost my job, and for that, I was incredibly thankful.

After the lieutenant had finished, I sat there quietly for a moment. I apologized for my conduct and I told him that I had accepted Jesus Christ into my heart and that he would *never* have to worry about misconduct from me again. I thanked him for his time, accepted the keys for my marked 2010 Ford Crown Victoria Police Interceptor, and walked out the door of his office.

I drove my unmarked stealthy Ford Police Interceptor around the building one last time as I hunted for my slightly used ride. It had been a few years since I had driven a Crown Vic, but I knew I could get used to it again. I was in a state of mental shock as I pulled up to yesterday's flagship of Ford police muscle. A thick layer of pollen gave the old Crown Vic the appearance of an Easter egg colored taxi. After jumping the slightly dead battery (always carry a set of jumper cables), I absentmindedly began to transfer all of my gear from the sleek shiny curves of the unmarked car to the boxy confines of the old Crown Vic.

What am I going to tell Stacy? A new panic overtook me. *Thank you, Lord, I did not lose my job! But I'm starting midnight shift in less than thirty-six hours and I'm about to drive home in this marked cruiser! I'll have to tell her. But maybe, maybe I don't have to tell her the real reason why I'm being sent to midnights.*

I didn't want to deceive my wife any more. I wanted the lies to stop. But I didn't want to tell her the truth either. I was too afraid, paralyzed with sickening fear to tell her the truth. How was I supposed to tell her that the real reason I was being disciplined was because I had been unfaithful? I knew it would break her heart, and

I didn't want to lose my wife and daughter. I was so ashamed and I felt so guilty for sinning against her, and Satan was using that guilt and shame to tell me that if I *did* tell her that I had been unfaithful, she would never forgive me. That would certainly be the end of my marriage and being a father to my daughter.

I wished that I could undo all the horrible things I had done when I had turned away from God. Things had just started to feel like they were slowly beginning to get better between Stacy and I, and I didn't want to destroy that hint of progress. And so even though I had given my heart and soul to Jesus, even though I had just been cleansed with baptism, I allowed Satan to justify the deceit. On the way home, I perfected what I would say.

It was around 4:00 p.m. when I pulled into the driveway, the tired suspension creaking on the old Crown Vic as I turned in. It was summertime, and Stacy was home from her job as a teacher. I was coming home a little earlier than usual, and I crept in like a dog with his tail between his legs. Stacy looked beautiful as she greeted me in the kitchen, her face beaming as she looked up from reading a book to our five-year-old daughter, Ana.

"You're home early!" She smiled as she spoke. I tried to force a smile back, but my face was having none of it. Too many secrets loomed within my heart. *Just tell her.*

"Yeah. We need to have a talk." *Let's just get this over with*, I thought to myself. "I got into some trouble at work. I'm going to midnight shift, permanently, starting tomorrow night."

Stacy stared at me in disbelief.

"What? How can that happen? You've worked so hard! You don't deserve that!" Stacy was confused and hurt. What she didn't know and what I was too cowardly to tell her was that I *did* deserve it. She pressed me for more details, but I remained tight-lipped. I led her to believe the discipline had something to do with a vehicle pursuit I had been involved in a while back. I told Stacy that there must be a reason for it, that we shouldn't question it, and I was okay with being assigned to nights because I was so burned out with all the death I had seen working fatal crash reconstruction.

As Stacy and I continued to talk about this life-changing turn of events, I walked into our bedroom. When we had added this bedroom on, over five years ago when Stacy was pregnant with Ana, Stacy had designed it beautifully with several windows that let in enormous amounts of daylight. There were French doors leading out to our back porch and a bay window looking out to the backyard. Above the bed were two smaller windows. When the sun came up, the sunlight would bathe the room with its brilliance.

As I entered the room, I couldn't help but notice how incredibly *dark* it was. It was as if I had just walked from day into night... strange. I stopped midsentence and looked around at the shrouded bedroom, wondering what was different. I asked Stacy what was going on and I couldn't believe her response.

Forgetting about our stressful, life-changing conversation for a moment, Stacy explained proudly that she had just finished putting up very dark "black-out" curtains in our bedroom to keep out the heat of the summer sun. To reiterate, she had just finished hanging the curtains—*that day*. She had *no knowledge* of the investigation I had been the subject of since I had been too gutless to tell her any of it. She absolutely had *no idea* that I was going to be assigned to work night shift, which meant I would have to sleep during the day. Anyone who has ever worked night shift knows how crucial it is to have a dark room to sleep in while the world ticks by outside. Without a dark room to sleep in, the human body cannot produce as much melatonin as it needs for healthy sleep. All I could think of was God and His mercy. Only God. God knew what was going to happen to me and so He orchestrated a room in which I would be able to sleep.

Stacy and I had very little time to process this whole thing as I started midnight shift the following night. I hadn't worked the night shift since 2008, exactly seven years prior. It certainly took some getting used to, to say the least. Just like that, my life was turned upside down again. This time, it was my own fault. I didn't know what my life was going to look like moving forward. I prayed that I would be able to tell my wife the truth.

Thus began a very difficult summer of uncertainty. My first night on midnight shift was the last Saturday night in June 2015. I tried to lay down for a couple of hours before my shift began at 10:30 p.m., but my mind was running wild with thoughts of anxiety. What would the other officers think? Were they all talking about me behind my back? Would they all hate me for being unfaithful? Surely they would know. Cops can't keep secrets amongst themselves; it's just a fact of life.

On that first night, I remember driving down the road, and every mailbox looked like it could be a person or a deer. I prayed my eyes would adjust. I would have to be on midnight shift for a minimum of one year before I would even be considered for transfer, so I was going to have to get used to it. I was assigned to work the west side of the county, a lonely place at times, especially during the night. Many nights, I would be the lone officer covering 200 square miles of roads, homes, businesses, farms, wooded areas, lakes, mountains, and streams.

One of the first calls I responded to was a strong armed robbery of a local convenience store. It was around 1:00 a.m., and I was the first police officer on scene. While en route, I was given the description of the suspect—a white male who was getting into a white Jeep in the parking lot. More information was coming in as I was about to arrive on location, something about the suspect trying to carjack someone after the robbery. As I prepared to pull into the parking lot of the convenience store, I saw a white Jeep that was starting to leave the lot. Knowing this had to be the suspect's vehicle, I flipped on the blue lights on the Crown Vic and pushed my way through the last red light between the suspect and me.

Just as the white Jeep was about to exit the parking lot, I pulled into its path and blocked it in with my cruiser. Several people in the parking lot were waving their arms and pointing at the Jeep. I jumped out of my car about the same time a white male popped out of the rear driver side door of the Jeep Cherokee. Two other Hispanic males were in the front seats of the Jeep. The Hispanic males appeared to be cooperating and so I made the split-second decision to engage the white male who was likely the one who had attempted to rob the clerk of the store. The white male was acting somewhat nonchalant, trying to act as if he was not the guy I was after. I decided to try to play down the whole situation, hoping it was all a misunderstanding.

Maybe I had been off the street a little too long, because acting casual turned out to be a big mistake.

I asked the suspect what was going on and asked him who had tried to take something from the store. The suspect avoided eye contact and told me, "I dunno, some guy." *Red flag* number one. The suspect then tried to light the remnants of a cigarette with a cheap plastic lighter he was holding. After having some trouble with the faulty lighter, the suspect leaned in close toward me and said, "I'll trade you this lighter for your F*$#ING gun!" *Red flag* number two.

At that point, I realized I had more than enough to detain this guy in handcuffs. He matched the suspect's description perfectly, and he was talking crazy. I probably should have detained him a lot sooner.

"Hey, take it easy! Put your hands behind your back, you're being detained!" I ordered.

"*No!*" The suspect yelled and clenched his fists, locking his arms. And with that, I attempted to grab a hold of one of his arms. The suspect charged forward and, in doing so, knocked me to the ground like a bowling pin. The suspect was shorter than me by a few inches, but at my new stress induced feather weight of 170 pounds, he outweighed me by a solid seventy-five pounds. Just as he knocked me down, I saw another police officer pull into the parking lot. *Thank God.* Seeing what the suspect had done to me, the other officer ordered the male to the ground with Taser drawn.

A Taser is a defensive weapon that police officers carry as a way to subdue a suspect who is combative or violently resisting arrest. When a Taser is fired, a nitrogen propellant shoots two probes into the target (suspect). The probes are connected back to the Taser with wires that conduct the 50,000 volts. As long as both probes connect with the suspect, an electrical circuit is completed using the suspect's body as a conductor. I can say from personal experience that when the Taser is properly deployed, it is a very effective tool.

Years ago, when I was training to use a Taser, I had to be shocked with one before I was cleared to carry it. The thinking was that you had to know what the Taser could do to you if it you were fighting with someone and the Taser was taken away from you. The feeling is difficult to describe. Thankfully, instead of shooting me directly with the Taser, the instructor fired the Taser into the ground and picked up the probes to tape them to my back. I remember the probes were carefully taped to my upper left shoulder blade and my right rear torso—the more muscles in between the probes, the more effective the Taser would be. I was instructed to kneel to reduce the likelihood of injuries. When the instructor pulled the trigger while the probes were taped to my back, my reaction was instantaneous. The arcing of the electricity popped and cracked, and involuntary expletives spewed from my mouth as I felt my muscles contract violently. Intense focused pain washed over me as the electricity surged across my back. My body stiff as a board, I fell forward on my face, unable to move. It was like being wrapped in an electric cattle fence. I quickly decided that was enough for me! If I had to choose between being sprayed in the face with pepper spray and being shocked with a Taser, the choice for me would be a no-brainer—pass the pepper, please!

The suspect refused to comply, and the Taser was deployed. The suspect groaned in pain as his muscles involuntarily contracted and he fell to the ground with 50,000 volts coursing through his body.

As I placed the belligerent suspect in handcuffs, I realized how fortunate I had been in the timing of the other officer's arrival. There were other options on my gun belt (expandable baton, pepper spray) that I could have used to attempt to subdue the suspect, but he already had me at a disadvantage when he knocked me down. You don't want to be on the ground with a suspect standing over you. That's a scary place to be. What's more, I didn't have a Taser issued to me at the time. The only other option from the ground may have been my firearm. But thankfully, it never got to that point, because the other officer arrived at the exact right moment to save me. God was truly watching out for me.

Insane as that night was, midnight shift wasn't all bad. I was continuously amazed by the beauty and radiance of the sunrise. I felt a closeness to God as I admired His creation and the canvas He painted with infinite awe each morning. But as June turned into July, and July turned to August, I still had not been brave enough to tell my wife the sin I had committed against her.

I continued to go to Rich Newsome's men's group, and I continued to go to church when I wasn't working the night before, but I couldn't bring myself to surrender the last corners of my heart to the Lord. I had made a little bit of headway in cutting back on drinking, but I was nowhere close to being free from alcoholism—it was like two steps forward, three steps back. The powerful grip alcohol had on me continued to chain me down. God wanted to change me, to work in my heart, but I was still unable to fully trust that my heavenly Father would redeem every area of my life. I was like a boat trying to set sail on an epic voyage, but I was still tied to the dock.

One Sunday afternoon in August, God decided that He was done waiting for me to cut the dock lines. It was time to face the nightmarish fear I harbored in the back of my heart—that Stacy would find out the sins I had committed against her.

I was at home that sunny Sunday afternoon with Ana. Stacy was working her part-time job that she sometimes worked on the weekends. Suddenly, there came a knock on the door. Cathy, a friend and coworker of Stacy's, was waiting on the other side of the door when I opened it. She announced she was there to take Ana out for ice-cream. *What? I wasn't told. Strange…* While I was trying to figure out how I had forgotten such an important detail in the day's events, my mother pulled into the driveway, also unannounced. *What is going on?*

It turns out my mother had arranged for Cathy to come over to get Ana. My mother told me that I needed to go with her. I could tell by her tone this was serious. Immediately, I knew something was up. Suddenly feeling sick with worry, I tried to act like I had no clue what this was all about. *But I knew.* Cathy rushed Ana out the door as I sheepishly sat down in the front passenger seat of my mother's silver Honda Accord. I pressed my mother for details, demanding that she tell me what was going on. Ultimately ignoring all questions I shot her way, my mother made some small talk, asking me if I had been listening to some of the Christian music she had given me on an iPod. We rode in silence, other than my occasional protest of her not telling me why she was kidnapping me.

After the ten-minute ride, we pulled into the driveway of my mother's house. There in the driveway was Stacy's car. The sight of her car only confirmed the sickening fear that was twisting my stomach into knots. *She knows.* My heart began to pound like a stampede of rhinoceroses. This was a whole new kind of fear. I wanted to leap out of the car and run away as fast as I could. I had refused to take the obedient step to reveal my sin to Stacy, so God had revealed it. *God help me.*

17

Crisis

Reluctantly, I followed my mother into her house. She led me to her office where my wife was waiting, sitting amongst the pillows of a white wicker daybed. My mother wasted no time in explaining the reason for this gathering—this intervention. Stacy had been at work at her part-time job and happened to check her email while she was on a break. One of the emails she had sitting in her inbox revealed my sins against her. Someone believed she had a right to know what I had done, and so they packaged it for her in an email.

Now I have no right to protest the crude and horrid manner in which this life-altering, devastating message was delivered to my wife, because I had my chance to be the one to tell her and I failed—completely. The only Godsend here was that she did not open the email while sitting at her desk in front of a room full of her students. My wife's full-time job was as a teacher at a local high school, and I don't even want to think of her reading that email while she was in class.

One of my first reactions was rage. I felt like someone was trying to destroy my family. I took it as a personal attack on me and on my wife and daughter. Maybe I had no right to feel this way, but that did not change the burning anger deep within me.

As my mother's words brought my deepest fear from the back of my heart straight into the moment, her voice started becoming distant as my mind began to whir with thoughts of despair and defeat. My panic turned to shock as I faced the reality of what was happening. The little bit of control that I was trying to hold onto had now been taken away. I could not lie anymore. I had been found out and my sins were no longer hidden. I was exhausted with the secrets and the burden of keeping the shame of my infidelity inside my heart.

Stacy was heartbroken and she was justly angry. She had every right to be. How could we ever move past this? How could she ever forgive me? She wanted to know everything. I didn't want to hurt her, but I was done lying.

I don't remember how, but I ended up on the floor, my head hung in shameful regret. I could feel the fury radiating from Stacy's green eyes, although I avoided eye contact. I pleaded with her for forgiveness and I attempted to manifest that my infidelity was before I had accepted Christ and that my heart had changed. My mother offered quiet wisdom from time to time. I felt so awful, so guilty, and worthless. There was nothing I could say or do that would fix this. Only God could help me now.

We frantically tried to call anyone we could from the church. Voicemail after voicemail greeted us in our frenzied search. It seemed the entire church staff was unreachable in our time of need. Finally, we thought to call Rich Newsome. When he answered the phone,

I felt a bit of relief. I told him what had happened while he was on speaker phone. Rich listened quietly, and for an agonizingly long moment, there was silence. Just when I thought he had hung up or the phone had disconnected, Rich finally spoke in his calm, even-toned, reassuring voice.

"Well, Jonathan has been coming to men's group for a few months now and he's been a joy to have with us. I know this is a hard time for you now, and I know that Satan would love to see your marriage destroyed because of this." Rich's words seemed so distant, though I clung to them as the only lifeline I had in this storm. There were little words of comfort that Rich could offer, but he did pray for us and said he would see what he could do about getting a pastor to call us. I thanked Rich and hung up.

What seemed like eons later as the last bit of daylight crept below the treetops, I rode in the passenger seat of Stacy's car, trying to shrink into the leather seat cushion. Half expecting (and fully deserving) to be slapped across the face at any moment, I braced myself for anything that would come. It was pretty amazing that Stacy was allowing me to ride with her in the first place.

As we neared home, I wondered what would happen when we arrived. I wondered if I would be packing my bags and heading back over to my mother's house. Just as I was pondering my eviction, a phone call came in to Stacy's cell phone. Stacy answered it using the Bluetooth in the car.

"Hi, is this Stacy? This is Dave Herring. I'm a pastor with the church."

The familiar voice gave me some comfort. Stacy started unloading everything and she didn't hold back. Her words were filled with resentment and desperation. As Stacy detailed what I had done, I listened to see what Pastor Dave would say. Pastor Dave was the only person I had told of my sins against my wife, and he had encouraged me to be honest with her. I'm sure this news came as no surprise to him.

Pastor Dave heard Stacy out and waited for her to finish. Pastor Dave mentioned that I had told him about the infidelity. He also told us that Satan would love for our marriage to be destroyed and right now, we needed counseling and prayer—*big time*. Pastor Dave arranged a time for Stacy to meet with him and his wife and assured us that he would send us a list of recommended faith-based counselors. He even said that the church would *pay* for us to see a faith-based marriage counselor!

Pastor Dave's timing was perfect and no doubt arranged by God. Just as we were on our knees with desperation, he called us. We were two minutes away from our driveway when the call came in and we were able to pull into the parking lot of a church near our home to take the call. After talking to Pastor Dave, we felt like we had some sort of plan to move forward, instead of churning our gears in the storm just to stay afloat.

After speaking with Pastor Dave for about fifteen minutes, he prayed for us. We thanked him for his time, and the phone disconnected. A cold silence filled the car. I did not feel it was my place or my right to speak.

Stacy finally spoke with reverent authority. "I am not going to kick you out of the house. I feel like God is telling me not to do that, if nothing else, for our daughter. But you *will* be on the couch."

I did not argue. I had no rights here, no say in the matter. Humility filled my heart. With that, we drove the rest of the way home.

After Stacy had gone to bed, I sat on the couch in the dark, drinking a beer as usual. With the horror of the day, normally I would have been desperate to drink heavily until I passed out. But I was so sick from what had happened, I had suddenly lost the desire to drink the beer. I could hear Stacy crying from our bedroom, sobbing in the undeserved grief I had placed upon her. As I nursed the longneck bottle, the symbol of the prison of alcohol that had enslaved me for over ten years, I suddenly heard a voice speaking to me.

"Stop drinking and change your ways or *I will* take everything from you."

I put the bottle down. I had never heard a voice so clear, so sure. This was not a still, small voice; this was my last warning. *God, please take this from me*, I prayed. *I fully surrender to you, Lord. Please save me.*

I had been a slave to alcoholism for so long. I had never been able to stop drinking on my own. After more than ten years of alcohol abuse, I was spending at least $250–$300 a month on beer, wine, and liquor to support my habit. I needed the alcohol so badly, I could not sleep without it. Being hung over was a daily occurrence for me.

The anxious feeling of needing to drink often plagued me. The few times I did try to quit drinking, the urges, cravings, and physical withdrawals were so powerful that I quickly succumbed to them. My body was fully dependent upon the evil elixir and its numbing properties.

That night, God answered my prayer. *God, please take this from me.* I didn't sleep well that night because of the nightmare-come-true that I had lived through that day. But the withdrawals did not control me, and I never looked back. This was a true miracle! By trusting God to save me, I was able to walk away from alcohol forever. Through His grace, I was saved and I never touched another drop of an alcoholic beverage.

The next day, I told Stacy about my drinking habit and how I had been hiding it from her for so long. She helped me, even in our state of absolute marital crisis, by removing all of the beer and wine from our home. It actually felt good to be able to tell someone who could hold me accountable.

In the book of Proverbs, it says "Guard the heart above all else, for it determines the course of your life" (Proverbs 4:23, NLT). Someone who is trying to stay away from drinking alcohol should not keep it in the house. Someone who is addicted to internet pornography should put a computer in a place where everyone can see it. If someone has a problem with gambling, they should stay out of casinos. And if you don't have the will power to control yourself, tell someone who will hold you accountable. That is how you guard your heart. God can help you with your temptation, but you can help yourself in certain ways too.

On my nights off from working midnight shift, I would often sit on the couch and try to distract myself with Netflix. After more than ten long years of drinking every night, I felt like my body still needed the ritual of holding a bottle—only now it was Perrier instead of Corona. Long after I thought my wife was asleep, she would suddenly walk in and ask me difficult questions about my sins against her. We would have long awkward talks while I squirmed on the couch and she stood distant from me with her arms crossed. I owed it to her to answer her questions honestly, and so I did. I did not wish to reveal details to her for fear of hurting her or angering her, but I knew that anything other than absolutely transparency would have only angered her further.

In order to be completely beyond reproach, I gave Stacy all of the passwords to my email, my iPhone unlock code, and my laptop. I also turned on my GPS sharing on the iPhone and shared it with our iPad so she could literally track me at any time she wished. These were necessary and important steps to take if she was ever going to be able to consider trusting me again.

I knew I was very fortunate to even be in the same house as my wife. On the days that I worked midnight shift, I was allowed to sleep alone in our bed. I remember sleeping in the bed alone for the first time since I had moved to the couch. I looked over at Stacy's empty pillow and was overcome with emptiness. I longed for the restoration of our relationship, but it would be in God's timing. Every day, I prayed on my knees before I would go to sleep with my hands laid on our bed. *Lord, please soften Stacy's heart. Please let her find it in her heart to forgive me. Please save our marriage, Lord. Thank you for saving me. Thank you for delivering me from alcohol. Not my will, Lord, but Thy will.*

Soon, I would get used to sleeping on the couch. I made sure to set the alarm on my phone early enough every morning so that my sweet five-year-old daughter would not come out of her bedroom to discover me sleeping on the couch and start asking questions. I did everything I could to serve my wife. I would make her breakfast in the morning and take care of packing Ana's lunch for kindergarten. It didn't make Stacy want to be around me, but it made me feel a little better to be able to do small things to serve her humbly.

As the time began to tick by, following the catastrophic Sunday that my sin was revealed to my wife, we struggled to find a faith-based counselor. It seemed like all of the counselors we reached out to had a minimum thirty to forty-five day wait before they could see us. To us, that was an absolute *eternity*. We needed a marriage counselor and we needed one yesterday.

On Tuesday of that week, Pastor Adam (who had baptized me a couple of months' prior) emailed me a list of faith-based marriage counselors. He affirmed that Stacy and I should continue to do what it took to press on in our marriage together. Pastor Adam generously offered that the church would provide scholarships for the counseling fees if we could not afford them. Soon I was looking at a list of several qualified counselors to choose from. I tried calling every name on the list. One receptionist told me that we could have an appointment in three weeks. Another counselor never returned my call until two days after I left a voicemail. Every door seemed to be closing in my face, and I was getting impatient and frustrated.

Sometimes God closes doors (in our face, if necessary) if they are leading us down the wrong path so that we will step through the right door. God opened the door he wanted Stacy and me to step through when I called Lynn Schwenk. Lynn, who just so happened to be the wife of Pastor Adam, answered the phone personally when I called. What a beautiful example of how God works—a gifted, compassionate pastor is married to a godly woman who counsels other Christians. I told Lynn what Stacy and I were facing, and Lynn quickly responded that she thought she could help us. She set up our first appointment for the following Sunday! I got off the phone and rejoiced in the first glimmer of hope since we entered crisis mode. *Lord, You are my redeemer. Thank You, Father, for Your faithfulness.*

18

Restoration

Stacy and I rode in unnerving silence on our way to our first appointment with Lynn. I was hopeful, but I had no idea what to expect. The last time I had seen a counselor of any sort was back in the sixth grade. When I found out that my father had terminal cancer, I began to have behavioral issues immediately. I would act out in class and do anything for attention. I remember being pulled out of class by one of my teachers wanting to know why I was behaving in such an inappropriate manner. I tried to tell her that my dad was sick and I just ended up turning to tears, breaking down, crying right there in the hallway. I wound up with an appointment with Mr. Thomas R. Olson, the school guidance counselor at my elementary school in Rutland, Massachusetts.

Being only eleven years old, meeting with a guidance counselor gave me the impression I was in trouble for something. And since I felt I was being sent to Mr. Olson as a result of my behavior, to me it was only a logical assumption at the time. But once I began to sit down and talk with Mr. Olson on a regular basis, I began to really look forward to my time with him. I remember the loudspeaker in the classroom would crackle with Mr. Olson's calming voice as he asked my teacher to send me down to his office. It made me feel important, like I had a crucial meeting with a figure of influence.

Mr. Olson treated me like one of his own sons. He really was a friend to me and so much more. He was another godly father figure who God had appointed to watch over me. My father was stricken with the effects of radiation treatments and chemotherapy and was limited in his activities and mobility. Mr. Olson invited me into his home to spend time with his children. He also took me along to a church youth group camping trip in Maine. He even took my younger sister, Sarah, and I to see the Harlem Globetrotters at the Worcester Centrum. Our world needs more leaders and fathers like Tom Olson.

I remember driving for hours with Mr. Olson to the church youth group camping trip in Maine in the middle of winter. It was a weekend camping trip meant for fathers and sons, and Mr. Olson had agreed to take me because my father was too ill. We had no idea where we were going, only that the roads we were on seemed more like paths through the woods. As we continued into the Maine wilderness, we ran into a terrible blizzard. The snow was coming down heavily, and I wondered if we would make it at all or if we would freeze to death in the forests of Maine between civilization and the camp. The dazzling brilliance of the fresh snow was highlighted by the headlights of Mr. Olson's Fiat before fading into the night. Mr. Olson was calm and hardly seemed worried as he pressed forward in the blinding, heavy snow. I tried not to be afraid or show my fear, but inside I was scared. I wasn't sure where we were going and I wasn't sure how we would get there.

So much of my life before inviting Christ into my heart was like that car ride. So often I was faced with fear and uncertainty, wondering if I was going the right way and wondering if I would ever get to where I wanted to go. Without full trust in the Lord, I wandered and wondered, trying to trudge forward on my own while trying not to show my fear to others.

As Mr. Olson drove into the swirling icy flakes of uncertainty, he remained calm and collected, cool, and in control. He trusted that God would get us where we needed to go and found peace in God's divine protection. And soon, in the middle of the worst snowstorm I have ever seen, the little Fiat pulled into the camp unscathed and ready to unload its weary passengers.

After I accepted Christ, despite my longing to trust God with all of my brokenness, I had been reluctant to give all areas of my heart to the Lord. I had not given up drinking and I had not told Stacy the truth. Alcohol still owned part of my heart, along with deceit. But now God had revealed my sins and He had freed me from the heavy iron chain of alcoholism. Now God could blow wind into the opening sails of my heart as He began to break the chains that tied my heart down.

Stacy and I finally arrived at the gigantic First Baptist Church where Lynn had a small office in the basement. Years ago, I remember my high school graduation took place inside the same church. I led the way into the church, sure to hold the door for her. We were a bit early, and so we waited in a small room just outside Lynn's office.

While we waited, Stacy said to me, "You had better not hold anything back. You have to fix yourself before we can fix our marriage!" I winced, but she was absolutely right.

I love to see a restored classic car. Some of the most beautiful cars on the road today are the classics from the fifties and sixties, lovingly and painstakingly restored to all their former glory. Timeless favorites like Ford Mustangs and Chevy Bel Airs are representative of a simpler time gone by. When taking on a restoration project, the restorer seeks an old car with a solid body, the framework from which to build a new creation. Original parts are highly desired for the restoration to be as correct as possible. Once the car is rebuilt, it is given a glossy new coat of paint and becomes an iconic symbol of cool and class.

If the restorer begins the restoration of a classic car using old broken rusted parts, and then finishes the job with a nice coat of high gloss British racing green, it would completely defeat the purpose of the restoration. In the end, you wouldn't have a final product worth much of anything! On the outside it may look good, but inside it would just be rusty scrap.

The same held true with the restoration of our marriage. If *I* did not take the time to restore the broken parts of myself, there would be no point in attempting to restore the marriage. If Stacy and I tried to restore our marriage without restoring my brokenness, the marriage itself would quickly fall apart again because the damaged parts were never repaired.

After we waited for a few minutes, Lynn came out of her office to introduce herself. Lynn is a sweet, quiet, reserved woman with a warm and reassuring presence. Stacy and I sat down in her cozy office, which was decorated with black and white pictures of what I guessed to be Manhattan. There was a black and white picture of a huge clock and another picture with some skyscrapers and some taxi cabs. There was a box of tissues ready to wipe away tears and a basket filled with hard candies. *Candy?* I liked Lynn already.

The floor was mine. I told Lynn everything and I didn't hold anything back as she typed notes on her iPad. I told her how I had lost my father when I was twelve and how I had moved to Virginia a few months later. I told her of all the death and brokenness I had seen as a police officer, the anger I had always felt inside, the alcoholism, the loss of my son Christian, the lust, the pornography, the infidelity, the darkness. I told her of my turning to the Lord and my acceptance of Christ and my failure to tell Stacy of my sins against her. By the time I finished, sure that I had already used up our whole appointment, I looked up to see if Lynn was still listening to me.

Lynn sat there quietly and patiently to be sure I was finished. She did not seem repulsed or disturbed. She was not taken aback or offended. Her first response acknowledged the loss I had faced.

"You've seen a lot of loss. I'm actually surprised you're doing as well as you are," Lynn said with understanding in her voice. Her words caught my attention. I didn't think I was doing so well, but perhaps Lynn had seen a lot worse.

Lynn remained positive and reinforced that she thought she could help Stacy and me, because I had accepted Christ and was repentant. She really believed in the power of Jesus and her belief helped Stacy and me to believe. This began several months of weekly appointments with Lynn, often meeting for double sessions (two hours). The time together was healing, but it was a slow process that took patience and absolute humility. I continued to pray every day that God would help Stacy to forgive me.

During one of the therapy sessions with Lynn, I poured my heart out about how much I hurt inside from the devastating loss of my father. I told her that I never felt like I got to tell him I loved him, that I really, *really* loved him. I also told her about a time that I always thought about with my father that gave me incredible aching guilt.

When my dad was fighting his cancer, I remember going to play with some friends after school without his permission. I was eleven years old and I rode my bike pretty much wherever I wanted to. Our town was small, and I could ride to almost anyone's house. On this particular afternoon, instead of coming home, I rode to a friend's house when I knew I shouldn't. I finally rode my black and white BMX bike home and parked it in the garage. I walked into the house and found my father waiting for me. I remember he was sitting in a blue upholstered chair near a window.

"Where have you been?" Dad asked me.

"Oh, uh, I've been home for a long time! I was playing outside in the woods behind the garage!" I lied.

"Your bike wasn't in the garage. I checked." Dad had caught me in my lie.

"Oh, well, I left my bike in the woods behind the garage! I better go get it!" More lies. And so I strolled outside and walked out to the garage, where I proceeded to wheel my BMX out of the garage and push it into the woods behind the garage. Man, this was good. I was a genius! Dad would never know! After plopping my bike onto the ground behind the garage, I walked a circle around it, picked it back up, and wheeled it back into the garage as if the bike had been in the woods all along.

"Okay, I put my bike away!"

I confidently walked back into the living room where my father was still sitting in his blue chair. "Jonathan, I watched you take the bike out of the garage. You lied to me!"

I could see the pain in my father's eyes. And that's all I remember. And so while I don't remember what happened next, what I do remember will always be in my heart.

He was sick, fighting the illness that would take his life, and I was being untruthful and deceitful with him. And I had never forgiven myself for it. How it made me hurt so deeply inside for what I had done to my father! What kind of person does that to someone, especially their father, especially when their father is dying? How could I have done such a horrible hurtful thing?

Lynn told me that we were going to try an exercise called the Empty Chair. At the same time that she told me the name of the exercise, I looked at the empty chair next to her. I almost knew what she was going to say—she wanted me to pretend that my father was sitting in that chair! *No way.* Not only was that ridiculous, I thought, but what would it accomplish? It seemed silly and I let Lynn know I didn't think it would be a very effective exercise. But Lynn was persistent that it would help, and I suddenly remembered that I needed to fix me before we could work on restoring our marriage and so I put on my humble hat and went ahead with the exercise.

I tried to remain open-hearted as Lynn explained that I was to look at the empty chair in front me and speak to the chair as if my father was sitting in it. She told me to speak to my father as if he were sitting right there in front of me, to use this opportunity to say all the things I wanted to say to him.

As I stared at the empty white upholstered armchair, I began to imagine my father sitting there. Suddenly, I was overwhelmed with emotion and sadness, and as I tried to begin to speak, the tears began to flow. It was too real. I *really* felt like he was sitting there in front of me. With my wife sitting next to me and the tears of sorrow streaming down, I began to talk to my dad.

"Dad? I just want to tell you how much I miss you. I wish that you hadn't died. I wish you were still here. I wish you had been here to see me graduate from the police academy… and get married, and… I wish you could meet my daughter, Ana. And I wanted to tell you that I'm sorry for lying to you on that day when I went back and pulled my bike from the garage. I'm sorry I hurt you. Dad… Dad, I wanted to also tell you that I love you. I don't feel like I told you enough. I love you *so much,* Dad."

After the exercise was over, I was quiet for a while, wiping the onslaught of tears and thinking about my father. Unbelievably, I felt better. I felt like all that guilt I had been carrying around inside of me, all of those unspoken words that I so longed to speak to my father, had finally been released. Wow. The power of a simple healing exercise humbled me. What I had almost dismissed as a waste of time turned out to be an extremely amazing experience.

As the counseling sessions continued, I looked forward to the time that Stacy and I were able to spend with Lynn. She had some very effective techniques and we began to make some incredible progress. Through prayer and trust in Jesus Christ to help restore our marriage, we began to dive into the deepest reaches of brokenness and conflict that had once turned my heart to stone.

The single most unifying "exercise" that Lynn asked us to try was praying together every night. We were a bit reluctant at first; we had never prayed together before. Prayer was always something that you did in your head and never out loud. Sure, I had prayed a few times in the men's Bible study group I had been attending, but never with Stacy. Lynn assured us it would be good for the restoration of our marriage, and so we accepted our homework assignment. Stacy and I prayed together that night, speaking out loud to the Lord, and began to pray every night together. The more we prayed together, the easier and more natural it was.

As the weeks turned into months, Stacy and I began dating each other all over again. As I fell deeper into darkness, our relationship had become more and more damaged and had been decimated to smoldering ruins. Now we had to rebuild the rubble, brick by brick. I remember the first time she allowed me to hold her hand, walking back to the car in the church parking lot after one of our appointments with Lynn. It was the absolute most wonderful feeling! For months, I hadn't been allowed to touch her at all. I longed for her physical touch and to be able to gently hold her hand in mine filled me with joy.

We began to go on miniature dates after our counseling sessions, usually going out for ice-cream. It had been so long since I had really been able to just sit down with my wife and appreciate her for who she was. Sometimes we would just sit there eating our ice-cream, no words were needed. The simple pleasure of sitting together was enough for me.

We went in for double sessions every Sunday for about five months. And while we *were* making progress, it was not all sunshine and rainbows. Stacy was crushed as a result of my sins against her, and we were in an extremely painful, arduous season. I remember one Sunday while the devastating wounds to Stacy's heart were still fresh. We were getting ready to go to church. I had gone into the bedroom to get dressed for church and suddenly encountered Stacy in the hallway. We were physically closer to each other than we had been since we went entered the storm.

"*You don't even touch me!* You stay *away* from me!" Stacy drew back as if she had been bitten by a rattlesnake. I immediately retreated away from her to give her space. I went back into the bedroom and fell to my knees in prayer. *Help me, God, please!* As I prayed, Stacy walked into the bedroom a few minutes later.

"I want to go to church with you," I pleaded.

"Fine, but you're riding in the backseat. I don't want you *near* me," Stacy shot back. I deserved it and I deserved so much worse. I rode in the backseat to church, sitting next to Ana in her booster seat. Ana delighted in the fact that Daddy was sitting with her in the back of the car.

During the time that we were seeing Lynn, we faced many tests. I struck a deer in my Volkswagen Passat on the way to Rich Newsome's men's group one evening in October. Stacy was backing out of a parking spot at a local McDonald's while she was getting a milkshake with Ana one afternoon after school, and a reckless driver in the parking lot smashed into her car causing thousands of dollars in damage. I went to a training event for work one day and was told I couldn't stay due to the fact that I was out of dress code. It was my fault and I should have just gone home and changed. Instead, I lost my temper and cursed and yelled, making a fool of myself in front of a room full of coworkers. I ended up getting suspended without pay for a couple of days. Stacy was written up at work for an innocent oversight. I was written up for missing court. Satan did not want to see our marriage restored and he was using his full arsenal against us as we desperately tried to work toward healing.

The Bible says, "Husbands, love your wives as Christ loved the church and gave himself up for her" (Ephesians 5:25, ESV). Before I had accepted Jesus Christ into my heart, I thought I had loved my wife, but I never loved her in the way God commands. I had sinned against her and she would have been on solid biblical ground to divorce me for good. But God had a different plan. Through the guidance of our faith-based counselor and through the healing power of Jesus Christ, Stacy and I completed our sessions with Lynn in just over four months. Four months! It was painful and it was humbling, but it was needed. It helped me as a person to work through so much of the unresolved pain and anger I had harbored in my heart. As my wife says, "If counseling isn't extremely difficult, it isn't working." I am blessed to have married such a godly woman who is wise beyond her years.

Unified in Christ, our marriage was *completely and miraculously* restored. Amazingly, we found ourselves more in love with each other than ever before. God had answered all of my prayers. Against all odds, Stacy forgave me for my sins against her and she was able to slowly begin to establish trust in me. With Jesus Christ at the head of our renewed matrimony, we were now a force to be reckoned with; and through the power of God's restoration, Satan's attempts to completely and absolutely destroy us had failed.

19

Jehovah Remembers

The Christmas of 2015 was my first Christmas in over ten years that I wasn't worried about when I would be able to drink. Our little family, with Ana now six years old, was just beginning to heal from the years of damage that I had allowed to spread in our home like a ravenous disease. I felt so incredibly free without the heavy iron chains of alcohol and I graciously thanked God in every prayer for freeing me from my prison. As time wore on, I was also able to completely walk away from my smokeless tobacco habit as I prayed that God would take it from me.

The more I completely trusted in the Lord, the more I saw His faithfulness. One by one, the enslaving chains that weighed so heavily upon my heart were broken, snapped like a taut fishing line with a 2,500-pound great white shark thrashing on the hook. *Doubt. Uncertainty. Anger. Lust. A wicked tongue. Slander. Jealousy. Despair. Pride. Greed. Deceit. Hatred. Fear*—as I was freed from these chains, the Lord was able to guide me for His glory.

That Christmas as I found new meaning in celebrating the birth of my Lord and Savior, Jesus Christ, I felt the Lord calling me to serve in the church. I had a desire in my heart to serve others and become part of making this wonderful house of worship happen, to be a contributor to honor my communion with Jesus. I went back to Connection Point, the little kiosk where one goes with questions on how to get started on, well, pretty much anything related to the church. Enthusiastically, I signed up to volunteer for two of the three Christmas Eve services.

My volunteer service with the church began with coffee and Christmas trees. Because I had no clue how to help in any capacity as a new volunteer, I was assigned to making coffee. No problem, I could do coffee—how hard could it be? Perhaps it was harder than I thought, because I soon found myself reassigned. Next, I found myself tasked with taking all of the ornaments off of one of those pre-lit artificial Christmas trees that the church had used for some festive decoration in the lobby area during the services.

I managed to get all of the 144 ornaments into some sort of box or bag, breaking only a minimal sacrificial amount. Right. Covered in tinsel (that stuff sticks to you like silly string), I now had to figure out how to get the tree disassembled and neatly placed into a box looking roughly the size of a shoebox. It was challenging, and I wasn't so certain the church would be able to use the tree again the next year, but I got it in the box! I wasn't going to let that little (festive) fake tree get the best of me.

Luckily for the church's decorations, I was soon able to join the ushering team in the following weeks. I thought the ushering team was an exciting assignment! I remember when I was little, watching my dad as he helped to take up the offering. He would pass those big golden saucer-like plates around the pews in the church. After passing the offering plates back and forth, he would gather with the three other elders in the back of the church. They would all walk together, almost like a small band of marching soldiers, holding the golden saucers like they were dinner plates toward the altar to present the offering. I admired and loved my father and I thought it was so cool *my* dad was taking up the money for the church. And so I was very proud to serve as an usher.

Unfortunately, ushering didn't exactly come naturally to me. I would always get nervous that I was going to foul up passing the offering basket to a row of people who had already received it from the other usher or even worse skip a row of seats *completely*. I would also worry that people wouldn't like where I seated them or that I wouldn't be able to find enough empty seats for a larger group of people. I also found that I couldn't turn off the vigilant cop inside of me. As I greeted everyone, I found myself visually scanning their waistbands and pockets for weapons or telltale bulges.

After a couple of months as an usher, I began to inquire about the church's safety team. Being a police officer, I was quickly accepted to the team and I hung up my usher's hat. I truly felt a strong calling from the Lord to help develop this team to better protect the church. I began learning the operations of the team and was absolutely eager to make suggestions. Within a few months of joining the safety team, I was asked to prayerfully consider joining the team permanently and taking the role as team leader. I hardly thought of myself as a leader. I prayed about the decision for a while. The more I thought and prayed about it, the more I knew this was what God wanted me to do. I decided I had better listen to what the Lord was telling me as I heard Him very clearly saying, "Trust Me."

God was using me in other ways too. Aside from my leadership role in the church, He was using me as a leader amongst my peers at work to mentor new officers. I began to look at the spiritually lost people I came across differently, treating them with more compassion and letting the new light of Christ within me shine. God was also using me as a spiritual example in my family. After I was baptized in June of 2015, my younger sister, Sarah, was baptized on October 5, 2015; and my older sister, April, was baptized on October 16, 2016. It was truly amazing to see the Lord at work in my life as I placed all of my trust in Him.

My life at home was beginning to be filled with trust, joy, happiness, and growth. As I continuously prayed for God to fully restore me and my family, I was seeing how great His faithfulness was. It was the first time since childhood that I could ever remember being really, *really* happy. This joy could only come from God as the Grand Canyon size hole in my heart was finally filled with what had been missing—Jesus.

As my heart became more filled with the light of Christ, I could see it reflected in the happiness of my wife and daughter. Sensing the tension in our marriage prior to God's miraculous restoration, my daughter Ana had begun to have behavioral problems in school and was a child filled with confusion, anger, and sorrow. As Stacy and I showed Christ's love to each other, Ana's heart was also restored. Now I could see the joy in Ana's sweet heart shining for all to see! Praise our God in heaven, for He loves us so!

A week before Easter Sunday of 2016, my family and I were enjoying an afternoon together at home. Stacy was helping Ana to learn to read by sending her on these fun little scavenger hunts around the house. Ana would be given a clue that was written on a piece of paper, which gave the location of the next clue. As she made her way to the secret places of all of the clues, she would end up with a small prize at the end—a piece of candy or a small toy. It was a creative way to help Ana have fun while she was learning to read. This is why Stacy is a rock-star parent and teacher with her many gifts and creative learning ideas.

While Ana was chasing clues all around our house, Stacy gave me a piece of paper. I opened it up, inquisitive. The paper read, "This is a scavenger hunt for *you*. Your next clue can be found on a yellow bear that has a cub."

A yellow bear that has a cub? This was too easy! But I was having fun already. I ran to the garage and found the next folded up clue lying on the seat of my bright yellow Cub Cadet lawn mower. I followed the clues, racing from one to another like a little kid, drawing nearer to whatever prize lay at the end of my treasure hunt. Finally, the last clue read, "Something waits for you in a safe place." I had to think about it for a moment. Could she mean…? I dashed to our bedroom where we keep a small safe. I hadn't opened the thing in months, and there really wasn't anything in there. I remember hoping the batteries inside the fingerprint recognition lock weren't dead. I pushed my thumb to the scanner, and after a familiar electronic "*Beep!*" the lock opened and the door of the safe popped open!

Eagerly looking inside the safe, my heart began to pound as I saw what was lying inside. A small, white, pen-sized object lay nestled in the felt on the bottom of the safe. I knew exactly what it was and I slowly reached for it. The anticipation in my heart was almost too much. It was one of those instant pregnancy tests, and inside my heart, I already knew why Stacy had wanted to make it fun to find it—she was expecting a baby!

I was so overwhelmed with joy! I ran to Stacy and swept her up into my arms. An onslaught of questions rapid-fired from my lips. I was beside myself with pure joy and excitement! This was an *amazing* Easter miracle from the Lord. Jesus said, "But if you remain in me and my words remain in you, you may ask for anything you want, and it will be granted" (John 15:7, NLT)! The restoration in my life was unbelievable, praise God from whom *all* blessings flow!

A week later on Easter Sunday, we revealed the news to the rest of our family. We placed a piece of paper inside one of the several dozen plastic Easter eggs that Ana dashed about picking up during a much anticipated egg hunt. This wasn't just any egg; along with the life-changing message it contained inside, this was the highly desirable *golden* plastic egg that every child loves to find during Easter egg hunts. All of the other eggs had been filled with jelly beans and other candies and small toys. We all gathered around the kitchen table after the egg hunt as Ana tore through her bounty. As Stacy's parents and my mother looked on, Ana popped open the golden egg. The little piece of paper fell out, and Ana picked it up.

"What does it say, Ana?" everyone seemed to ask her at once.

Ana carefully unfolded the slip of paper and read the words, "I'm going to have a little brother or sister!" The joy of this moment was so pure as we all rejoiced in the wondrous miraculous revelation.

As soon as I found out that Stacy was expecting, I began to pray for the protection of this unborn child. Stacy and I were certainly concerned over the pregnancy after the devastating loss of Christian. Her ob-gyn had told her that she was now considered "high risk" after the tragedy we experienced. I immediately took the news of our pregnancy to my men's group. These righteous men of Christ had diligently prayed over my marriage when Stacy and I had gone into crisis, and now I wanted these prayer warriors to cover this pregnancy in prayer. Once the men's group began praying for the health of this unborn child, I felt a great peace as I heard God saying, "Trust Me."

As the weeks progressed, we began a new series of sermons at church entitled *The Circle Maker.* The series was based upon an amazing book with the same title by Mark Batterson. The entire church was provided with the book to read. The sermon series title and content was certainly timely as the church had to move into the school gymnasium due to the auditorium being unavailable. The gray metal folding chairs had all been arranged in a circle on the gym floor; the band played and Pastor Gabe preached in the center.

One Sunday in early May of 2016, I sat in one of the chairs in the big circle, listening to Pastor Gabe teach one of his messages based on *The Circle Maker.* Stacy and I did not know if our new baby would be a boy or a girl, and our appointment was coming up soon. With Ana, we waited to find out the gender of the baby until she was born. We decided we didn't want to wait with the new baby. That was fun *once,* but knowing ahead certainly has its advantages.

As Pastor Gabe spoke, he began reading from the book of Zechariah. He spoke about praying circles around what you are asking God for and how to pray boldly through it—no matter how big or small. He explained that Zechariah means, "Jehovah Remembers." Pastor Gabe read from Zechariah, "Not by might, nor by power, but by my Spirit, says the Lord of hosts" (Zechariah 4:6, ESV). In other words, anything is possible, but not by might, the resources of people, and not by our own power—but only by the Spirit of God. In that moment, I knew that if God blessed me with a son, he would be named after Zechariah to serve as a constant reminder of God's grace, power, and spirit.

The Circle Maker series was very personal to me as I began to boldly pray circles around the health of this unborn child. I trusted God would hear my prayers and protect this precious life. A few weeks later, Stacy and I learned what I already felt in my heart would be true—we were, in fact, being blessed with a new baby boy. I told Stacy that I felt God was telling me what his name would be, and we quickly agreed on a slight variation of the spelling: Zachariah.

God heard and answered our prayers, and the pregnancy was completely healthy and flawless. Early in November 2016, Zachariah arrived right on time. Stacy was beginning to have contractions at home, but they were coming inconsistently. The doctor's office told Stacy to come in to the office and they would check to see how far she was dilated. I was a bit on edge, not wanting to risk the health of our child or the health of my wife. We packed a bag, and my mother and we headed to the doctor's office. As we began the twenty-minute ride to the doctor's office, the contractions started coming at a much quicker rate. Every five minutes, then every three minutes! It was like the car ride acted as a catalyst for my wife's labor. It was a Toyota Highlander, if anyone is looking for a vehicle that will speed up labor—just kidding. When the contractions started coming every three minutes, we were sitting at the bottom of the exit ramp to the doctor's office. I heard that still small voice very clearly, "Go to the hospital." I shot right back onto the bypass and headed for the hospital. I wasn't messing around, and I knew this was the right move.

We pulled into the hospital and got Stacy right into a delivery room—it was almost like a scene from a movie. A nurse checked her, and Stacy was already dilated to seven centimeters (at nine centimeters, it's time to start pushing)! Within two hours, at 3:14 p.m., Zachariah Jonathan Gordon Hickory was born. Stacy actually pulled him out of the womb and into her arms. He was so incredibly beautiful, and my eyes filled with tears of joy and rejoicing. My heavenly Father had blessed us with this amazing beautiful son.

Holding the sweet baby boy in my arms for the first time, I was overcome with thankfulness for how God had turned my life out of the absolute pits of darkness and death and used all the suffering and emptiness for His glory.

"The steadfast love of the LORD NEVER CEASES; his mercies never come to an end; they are new every morning; great is your faithfulness. 'The LORD IS MY PORTION,' says my soul, 'therefore I will hope in him'" (Lamentations 3:22–24, ESV).

Six weeks later, I found myself looking across a laminate topped sea-foam green table at Pastor Dave as he and I replayed the events of my life over scrambled eggs, bacon, and short stacks of pancakes at a favorite local diner. Amidst the clattering of dishes from the kitchen in the background and the bustle of the breakfast crowd, Pastor Dave casually suggested that I should share my story, because it would bring people hope and show the life-changing power of Jesus Christ.

As I began to consider the idea, not really sure what he was getting at, he dropped the bombshell, "You know, we are looking for a powerful story to feature in a video for our Christmas church services coming up. Your story would bring hope to a lot of hurting people at a time when they need hope the most." Either Pastor Dave really had a way of selling things or the Holy Spirit touched me in that very moment, because instead of spitting out my coffee, I actually began considering the idea. Pastor Dave told me to think about it and he would check back with me soon.

The more I thought about the idea, the more the Holy Spirit encouraged me. I thought about all the married couples out there who had experienced the loss of a child and all of the people who have struggled with addiction or alcoholism or been affected by a family member battling substance abuse. I also thought about the couples affected by affairs and adultery. These were all things that no one wanted to talk about, and they were all things that Satan uses to destroy lives and marriages every day. I knew what to do.

When I told Stacy that I was planning on making a video with the church, she wasn't exactly jumping up and down to hop on this train ride with me. She had been through a lot and had gracefully forgiven even more, and understandably, she didn't want to let the world know it all. So I asked if we could soften the rawness of reality and take out the mention of the infidelity. After some thought, Stacy graciously agreed to help me tell our story.

Within a week, a small film crew of volunteers from the church was transforming our home into a backdrop for the video and the production was underway! When the filming and editing was complete, a powerful, emotional piece of videography was ready to be shared with the church for Christmas Eve. The video was played to over 1500 people during the three Christmas Eve services.

On New Year's Day, the video was released on the church's Facebook page. It was viewed an additional 2500 times—and counting—online! Despite the lurking fears of everyone knowing the road I had traveled, countless people reinforced the prompting of the Holy Spirit by thanking Stacy and I for telling our story. One man who I had never met before came up to me after one of the Christmas Eve services and hugged me! He and his wife had lost a child as well and he carried his sorrow with him every day.

Even today, when I pull up the video entitled *Hickory Life Change*, it brings me to tears. The seven-minute long video always rekindles grief, pain, sadness, darkness, anger, followed by salvation, joy, restoration, and redemption. While the viewer sees the miraculous and amazing life-change occur in seven minutes, for me it had taken years. The sadness, the depression, and the fear had gripped me for so long and robbed me of so much of my life. But the Lord pursued me relentlessly and He completely redeemed my life. For nothing is impossible for God, and there is no one beyond the hope of the life-changing power of Jesus. For if we let Him, He will take away the darkness that overwhelms our soul, and upon entering our heart, He will transform us forever.

20

Live for Him

My heart began to pound as I was introduced to over 300 students, ranging from seventh to twelfth grade, by The Covenant School's Bible teacher, John Collmus. I remember John was the assistant headmaster over twenty years ago when I attended. I have had the opportunity to speak in front of larger groups of people in the past—but as I looked out into the eyes of these children, I saw *myself* as a child. What if this was the *one* chance these young adults would get to be warned about the darkness and emptiness that comes with a life void of Jesus Christ? As the expectant young faces waited for me to begin speaking, I collected my thoughts and took a deep breath.

I began by reading the verse that I have found to be the best way to describe how I have seen God work in my life and in the lives of so many others. "And we know that God causes everything to work together for the good of those who love God and are called according to His purpose for them" (Romans 8:28, NLT).

As I began talking about the loss of my father and then the loss of Christian and all the darkness I used to dwell in, I struggled to hold back my tears and emotions. The brokenness of my past and the unsurpassable joy of my freedom and miraculous life-change in Jesus Christ provided an emotional roller-coaster ride as I spoke in front of these young impressionable teenagers.

I find that as time goes on, God is using me to pour light into the lives of others as I tell of the miracles God has woven into my life. He is constantly using the power of my testimony to bring encouragement to others and to bring hope to those walking in darkness.

When I think about the loss of my father as a child, I will never understand why my father died at such a young age, leaving his wife and children behind on this earth at a time when we needed him so much. I have found that the most faithful and thankfully easiest thing to do is to trust God and His master plan. We may not always understand why tragedies occur or why we are going through certain trials in our lives, but our heavenly Father knows exactly the reason behind every single moment, and He will work every moment together for our good.

Without Jesus, the sickening and sad reality is that I would be divorced with weekend custody of my daughter, and Zachariah would not exist. Without Jesus, I would still be chained down by anger, alcoholism, depression, and sin. Even worse, I might be dead, my soul forever burning in hell. This may seem extreme, but Jesus said, "I am the way and the truth and the life. No one comes to the Father except through me" (John 14:6, NIV). My soul didn't stand a chance.

Life is so, *so* different now. My eyes are wide open to the favor and the blessings that God has given me. As I watch my son, Zachariah, joyfully play with my daughter, Ana, I am constantly reminded of the undeserved grace I have been shown. My wife and I are closer than we ever were before with God as the sovereign head of our marriage. Stacy and I pray together every night; there is great power in our prayer time together! Instead of loathing each day, I look forward to my life which I now spend living for Jesus Christ. Every single day, I follow Him and ask God to help me to live for Him as I am called according to Jesus's own words: "You are the light of the world. A city set on a hill cannot be hidden. Nor do people light a lamp and put it under a basket, but on a stand, and it gives light to all in the house. In the same way, *let your light shine before others*, so that they may see your good works and give glory to your Father who is in heaven" (Matthew 5:14–16, ESV; emphasis mine).

Before Jesus Christ changed my life, I was living in agreement with the words of the enemy. *You're nothing but a worthless drunk. You are an angry detestable man, and there is no hope for you. You will never be happy.* I let Satan whisper in my ear and I wasn't willing to give my burdens to God for fear of relinquishing the control that I thought I had over my life. As I continued to live in a darkness that was absolutely void of God, the hole in my heart continued to grow.

As is so common for lost souls, I tried to fill that hole in my heart with anything of this world that would gratify me—lust, pride, material things, vanity, immorality. The problem with investing in nothing but ourselves is that in the end, the only thing that we will have to show for ourselves *is ourselves.* If we put our hope in anything other than Jesus Christ, it cannot and will not stand.

Without tiring, God mercifully pursues the lost sheep. Jesus said, "What do you think? If a man has a hundred sheep, and one of them has gone astray, does he not leave the ninety-nine on the mountain and go in search of the one that went astray? And if he finds it, truly, I say to you, he rejoices over it more than over the nine-ty-nine that never went astray. So it is not the will of my Father who is in heaven that one of these little ones should perish" (Matthew 18:12–14, ESV).

If you are the lost sheep, lost in darkness, and running far from your shepherd, He will relentlessly and lovingly pursue you. He pierces the darkness to save you! We are wretched sinners, worthy only of *death*—and the perfect Father wants us? His love is such an amazing, perfect love! Think of how much a mother or father loves their own children, and multiply that times the number of grains of sand on the seashore. Only then will you be able to begin to fathom just "how wide, how long, how high, and how deep his love is" (Ephesians 3:18, NLT). Remember the license plate?

One crucial thing I have learned in my experience about the character of God is that sometimes God will allow a crisis or some-thing traumatic to get our attention. C. S. Lewis once said, "Pain insists upon being attended to. God whispers to us in our pleasures, speaks in our consciences, but shouts in our pains. It is his mega-phone to rouse a deaf world." Five years ago, God was the last thing on my mind. I hated who I was, who I had become. I hated the life I lived, and I easily took every blessing God had given me for granted. Drowning in alcohol, anger, hatred, and depression, I refused to grab the lifeline God was laying before me.

God had been nudging me, trying to get me to take His gift of eternal life and peace. *I'm doing just fine, God! I don't need you!* I pushed Him away as I began to destroy myself—more alcohol, more anger, deeper into the darkness. And as I continued to turn away from Him, crisis soon found its way into my life with the loss of a child; and I still continued to run from God, even running harder, faster. Finally, I reached the end of the dark runway, dripping with the sweat and tears of turmoil and pain. The only two places at the end of the runway were heaven and hell. I had a choice to make. And by His grace, I was saved.

If God had created us without the freewill to choose a relationship with Him, we would simply be slaves, made to be obedient to His command. But God loves us because we are His children, His creation made in His own image. Just as *we* love our own children unconditionally, and desire a loving relationship with them, God deeply desires a loving relationship with us. If we had no choice in the matter, the love would not be real; the love would be programmed into us and we would be as robots, loving God only because we were forced to and without the depth of understanding. But we do have a choice, and when a sinner makes the decision to accept Jesus into their heart and form a relationship with God, the result is beautiful, genuine love for Him.

My friend, be encouraged! My life is just one of countless lives changed proving that with Jesus Christ, there is nothing so dead that new things cannot grow. The healing and restoration of our brokenness *begins* with trusting God fully with all of our hearts. "Therefore, if anyone is in Christ, he is a new creation. The old has passed away; behold, the new has come" (2 Corinthians 5:17, ESV).

God loves to turn the tables. It's one of the things He is absolutely the best at! But we have to be in a position of obedience, a position of readiness, where we are able *and* willing to receive what God has for us. If you are obedient to God, He will show you favor. Favor is God breaking the rules to bless us!

Psalm 23 is the most beautiful example of how the Lord can restore us, if we let Him.

> The Lord is my shepherd, I shall not want.
> (Psalm 23:1, ESV)

Jesus is the only one who will forever satisfy. God will fill that longing in your heart. I remember the daily unquenchable wants I had for alcohol, lust, prideful ambitions, and self-gratification. Now as I walk in obedience and trust with the Lord, He has reconditioned and restored my heart; Jesus Christ is the perfect cornerstone for the heart that God created.

> He makes me lie down in green pastures. He
> leads me beside still waters. (Psalm 23:2, ESV)

When we trust Him with all that we are, God will bring us to a place of rest. I no longer spend countless unsettled hours in restlessness. I no longer live in fear, plagued by anxiety and worry. I am a child of God and I know He is sovereign and has great plans for me.

> For I know the plans I have for you, declares
> the LORD, plans for welfare and not for evil, to give
> you a future and a hope. (Jeremiah 29:11, ESV)

> He restores my soul. He leads me in paths of
> righteousness for his name's sake. (Psalm 23:3, ESV)

God will fully restore you and your joy. With Jesus, I have a new inner light that shines brightly in the darkness of this world.

> Even though I walk through the valley of
> the shadow of death, I will fear no evil, for you
> are with me; your rod and your staff, they com-
> fort me. (Psalm 23:4, ESV)

He leads us into a place of relief, without fear, from the darkest of places. This fallen, broken world is filled with valleys and shadows, and the only place we can *always* turn is to God. His perfect love knows no limits, and He will bless us in our obedience when we trust Him fully.

> You prepare a table before me in the pres-
> ence of my enemies; you anoint my head with
> oil, my cup overflows. (Psalm 23:5, ESV)

We face enemies every day. Fear, anxiety, depression, addiction, conflict and turmoil. God will protect us and shepherd us, and deliver us. As we rest in the presence of the Good Shepherd, our enemies are forced to pass us by as they realize they cannot touch us.

> Surely goodness and mercy shall follow me
> all the days of my life, and I shall dwell in the
> house of the LORD forever. (Psalm 23:6, ESV)

Forever as in eternity! I have unlimited access to the presence of God at all times, because I now live in a constant state of praise and realization of His grace. I know that God loves me. When you know that God loves you, you live like you are loved. When you live like you are loved, people see the difference. They want to know, what is different about you? What is that light that shines from within you? As I continuously praise God for my miraculous restoration and life change, I give Him the glory and pray to lead others into a relationship with Him.

God has been writing and rewriting lives with miracles and restoration since the beginning; it's His specialty! Once we have allowed Him to form us into a new creation, how do we continue to survive on this bloody battlefield? Paul tells us in the book of Ephesians that the battles we fight are "not against flesh and blood, but against the rulers, against the authorities, against the cosmic powers over this present darkness, against the spiritual forces of evil in the heavenly places" (Ephesians 6:12, ESV). So yes, we must equip ourselves with the weapons and armor that God has provided for us—the belt of truth, the breastplate of righteousness, the readiness of the gospel of peace, the shield of faith, the helmet of salvation, and the sword of the spirit which is the word of God!

Recently I was talking to a good friend and coworker of mine, Curtis Kenney. Curtis knew me before I accepted Jesus Christ into my heart and has worked with me as an officer at the police department for fifteen years. Most importantly, Curtis is my brother in Christ. We were talking about the amazing power of God and how He restored my life and my family. We started talking about the trials of life and how a relationship with Jesus Christ gives us power over them. Curtis said to me, "The way I see it is this. Before, you had no armor. Even though you are still going to face tests and trials and attacks, now you *have* armor and you are *invincible* to the enemy." What an amazing truth! Equipping yourself with the armor of God is the only way to survive this ruthless world.

Survival

My friend, here is what has become my simple survival guide as a believer in Jesus Christ. ***The First Step*** to surviving the battlefield is to pray and pray often. We need to be in constant communication with God, and the objective of our prayer needs to be to align our will with God's will. The more we align our will with His, the more peace we will find.

Step Two: stay in the word! I'm not telling you that you need to pick up the Bible and read it cover to cover in one week. Start small if you have to, a verse or two a day if need be. Sign up for an email devotional or download an app that has daily devotionals on your phone. Spend time with God by reading and studying His word every day. I love getting daily devotionals in my email from Pastor Greg Laurie of Harvest Church. The more scripture you read, the more you learn about the character and unstoppable love of God.

Step Three of survival is to surround yourself with a community of other believers. We were designed by God to build each other up, pray for each other, and hold each other accountable. Go to church and pay attention to the teaching of God's word. Many churches have "small groups" or "life groups" or "community groups" that meet outside of the regular Sunday services. Find one, commit to it, and challenge yourself to participate! You may even surprise yourself and become a group leader. It is a blessing for your soul and it will nurture your spiritual health, I promise.

Step Four is to change your "diet." The more junk food you put into your body, the more fat you will gain, and the higher your blood sugar and cholesterol will be. So why would you continue to feed your soul junk as a believer? If you continue to listen to worldly music and watch TV that is filled with immoral depictions and filth, what do you expect the outcome will be for your soul? Instead of trash music blasting into your brain from the Top 40 radio station, listen to a Christian station. Instead of jumping in line to see the latest sex-filled violent movie, try something from a Christian streaming service. The Bible tells us, "Above all else, guard your heart, for everything you do flows from it" (Proverbs 4:23, NIV).

Step Five of survival is to stay in worship and praise of God at all times! Worship melts away worry and anxiety, and prayer gives us the peace of God that surpasses all understanding. Paul writes in Philippians, "Rejoice in the Lord always; again I will say, rejoice. Let your reasonableness be known to everyone. The Lord is at hand; do not be anxious about anything, but in everything by prayer and supplication with thanksgiving let your requests be made known to God. And the peace of God, which surpasses all understanding, will guard your hearts and your minds in Christ Jesus" (Philippians 4:4–7, ESV).

I will forever live for the Lord, for He has saved me from the darkness. He has broken every chain that enslaved me in bondage, and He has restored my soul, my marriage, my family, my very life. He has forever changed my eternity and the future of my children. I will praise my heavenly Father with all that I am and with every breath, for He pursued me when I was lost. The Good Shepherd, my all powerful Creator, from whom all blessings eternally flow, has given me the gift of life, and He will never let me down.

I pray that this story has touched you in some way and moved your heart, for it is truly a miracle that God has worked in my life.

For God alone, O my soul, wait in silence,
for my hope is from him.
He only is my rock and my salvation,
my fortress; I shall not be shaken.
On God rests my salvation and my glory;
my mighty rock, my refuge is God.
Trust in him at all times, O people;
pour out your heart before him;
God is a refuge for us.

—Psalm 62:5–8, ESV

Jonathan, 8 years old

Dad, Gordon E. Hickory

Jonathan's senior high school yearbook photo

Jonathan and Stacy, 2004

Academy Graduation

Daniel and his wife Adriane

Daniel smiling under his helmet

Christian's Memorial Marker

Christian's Memorial Tree, in full bloom

Jonathan's baptism, saved by grace

Sign 1-Ephesians 3:18

Sign 2-four leaves

Sign 3-in His timing

Jonathan, Stacy, Ana and Zachariah

Ana and Zachariah

About the Author

Jonathan Hickory is a master police officer with the Albemarle County Police Department in Charlottesville, Virginia. In his fifteen plus years of police experience, Jonathan has mentored and instructed other officers in police driving methods and as a field training officer.

Jonathan spent seven years investigating the reconstruction of fatal vehicle crash sites and three years as a motorcycle officer. He also leads a life safety team with The Point Church in Charlottesville. Jonathan has been married to his wife, Stacy, for over fourteen years and has two children, Ana and Zachariah.

CPSIA information can be obtained
at www.ICGtesting.com
Printed in the USA
BVHW071437190819
556217BV00003B/418/P